THE FIRST BOOK ABOUT CREDIT REPAIR

2026 Edition

DAN KOST

CEO, Money Smarts LLC

Founder of the Credit Repair Industry and Pioneer of the Credit Services Act of California, 1984

Money Smarts LLC | Dakdan LLC Media and Publishing | Colorado 80550,

THE FIRST BOOK ABOUT CREDIT REPAIR
2026 EDITION

Published by Dakdan LLC Media and Publishing through its Money Smarts imprint. Colorado 80550, USA
Cover Design:

Hardback ISBN: 978-0-916539-38-2
Paperback ISBN: 978-0-916539-39-9
eBook ISBN: 978-0-916539-40-5

First Edition was published in 1983 by Teltrans Credit Corp. Second Edition Published in 1985 by Teltrans Credit Corp, 2026 Edition published 2026. with Teltrans Credit Corp and Money Smarts, LLC

Cover design: Gary Maiers

Contents

A Note from Dan Kost vii
Introduction: How Credit Repair Works ix

Part One
The Foundation Strategy

1. The Credit Repair System: The Master Strategy 3
2. Your Credit Score: What it is and What it is Not 6

Part Two
Understanding the Credit Bureau System

3. The Big Three: Equifax, Experian, and TransUnion 11
4. How Credit Bureaus Build Your File 17
5. The Reporting Cycle and Timing Your Strategy 20

Part Three
The Law is on Your Side

6. The Fair Credit Reporting Act: Your Primary Weapon 27
7. The CFPB: The Bureau That Watches the Bureaus 31
8. Other Laws That Protect You 34

Part Four
Secondary and Specialty Bureaus

9. Beyond the Big Three: The Full Credit Ecosystem 39

Part Five
Credit Scores Explained

10. FICO, VantageScore, and the Scoring Wars 45

Part Six
Advanced Dispute Strategies

11. The Complete Dispute System 51
12. Dealing with Debt Collectors 56

Part Seven
Rebuilding Positive Credit

13. Building and Maintaining a Strong Credit Profile 61
14. Business Credit: Building a Separate Financial Identity 66

Part Eight
Special Situations

15. Identity Theft: What to Do When Your Credit is Hijacked 71
16. Credit and Housing, Employment, and Insurance 74
17. Bankruptcy and Credit: The Truth 77
18. Debt Restructuring: The Alternative to Bankruptcy 80
19. Credit as a Launch Platform: Houses, Businesses, and Careers 86
20. Getting Ready to Buy a House: The Complete Credit Preparation Plan 93
21. Negotiating with Creditors: Pennies on the Dollar and Full Deletion 98
22. Driving Records, Insurance Rates, and Your Right to Dispute 104

Part Nine
The Future of Credit

23. Where the Credit System is Headed 111
24. Your Action Plan: The Complete Step-by-Step Timeline 114

Appendix A: Complete Agency Contact List 117
Appendix B: Sample Dispute Letter Template 121
Appendix C: Glossary of Key Terms 123
Appendix D: Complete Directory of Consumer Reporting Agencies 127
Index 145

A Note from Dan Kost

In 1984, I wrote the first book about credit repair. At the time, nobody in America understood that credit reports contained errors, that those errors were harming real people, and that ordinary consumers had the legal right to fight back.

The credit bureaus did not want anyone to know that. They fought the industry at every step. They fought me personally. And they lost.

I was instrumental in passing the first Credit Services Act in California in 1984, which gave credit repair companies the legal framework to operate and gave consumers the framework to demand accuracy. That legislation became the model for what followed at the federal level.

Now, more than forty years later, the credit repair industry is a major sector of American finance. And the core truth I established in 1984 has not changed: your credit report can be wrong, those errors can destroy your financial life, and you have the right to fix it.

What has changed is everything around that truth. The system is larger, more complex, and more powerful than ever. There are now more bureaus, more scoring models, more data sources, more regulations, and more ways for errors to enter your file. But there are also more tools available to consumers who know how to use them.

This 2026 Edition, is the most comprehensive version of this book to date. It covers everything from the simple core strategy that still works today to the advanced regulatory landscape of today and beyond.

The foundation of credit repair is still the same: freeze every bureau you can find, dispute everything that cannot be verified, and remove what is not provable. That is it. Everything else in this book exists to help you understand why that works and how to execute it at a higher level.

Read this book. Then act on it. Your credit score is not a life sentence.

Dan Kost

Founder, Credit Repair Industry

Colorado 80550, USA

Introduction: How Credit Repair Works

Credit repair is not complicated, and it never has been. The industry made it seem complicated because complex things are easier to charge money for. This book strips away all of that and gives you the plain truth.

Here is how credit repair works in 2025, in plain English:

Step 1: Freeze your credit at every bureau you can find, not just the Big Three.

Step 2: Pull your credit reports and identify every negative item.

Step 3: Dispute everything that cannot be verified.

Step 4: What they cannot verify, they must remove. That is the entire system.

Everything else in this book is context, tools, and refinements built around that core process. The reason this works is rooted in federal law. The Fair Credit Reporting Act (FCRA) requires that every item on your credit report be accurate, complete, and verifiable. If a creditor or collection agency cannot verify that a debt is accurate and belongs to you, the bureau must delete it.

The credit bureaus hate this. The debt collection industry hates this. They have spent decades and millions of dollars lobbying to limit your rights. But the law is still the law, and it is on your side.

WHAT IS DIFFERENT TODAY

The biggest changes since the original edition of this book are these:

- There are now dozens of credit bureaus and specialty reporting agencies, not just three. You need to know about all of them.
- The Consumer Finance Protection Bureau (CFPB), created in

2010, now has direct supervisory power over the Big Three credit bureaus. That means real enforcement and real penalties.
- Credit scoring has expanded significantly. Fair Isaac Corporation (FICO) alone has over twenty versions in active use. VantageScore has become a legitimate competitor.
- Alternative data is now being used to build credit scores, including rent payments, utility bills, and bank account cash flow.
- The freeze strategy is now more powerful than ever because it forces bureaus and furnishers to verify data they often cannot verify.

The person who reads this book and applies the strategies inside will be better equipped to manage their credit than ninety-nine percent of American consumers. This is not an exaggeration. Most people do not know what a specialty bureau is, do not know they can freeze LexisNexis, or know that the CFPB complaint process is a legitimate escalation tool with real power.

Now you will.

Part One

The Foundation Strategy

Chapter 1

The Credit Repair System: The Master Strategy

Before we get into the details of credit bureaus, laws, and disputes, you need to understand the master strategy. This is the method I have taught and refined over forty years. Everything else in this book supports this core approach. I call it the Credit Repair System, and it has three phases.

PHASE ONE: LOCK DOWN THE SYSTEM

Before you dispute anything, you need to lock down every access point to your credit data. That means freezing your credit at every bureau that holds a file on you.

Most people know about the Big Three: Equifax, Experian, and TransUnion. But there are dozens of other agencies that report on consumers. Part Four of this book covers all of them in detail. For now, understand this: every bureau you leave unfrozen is a bureau that creditors and collectors can use to report negative data and pull your file without restriction.

When you freeze a bureau, the following happens:

- No new creditor can pull your file from that bureau without your permission.
- Prescreened credit offers based on that file stop.
- Certain kinds of data updates are restricted.
- The bureau cannot use your file in many of the ways it normally would.

Freezing does not hurt your credit score, nor does it prevent you from applying for credit. It gives you control. And when you are in dispute mode, control is everything.

Important note: Do not freeze the Big Three during the active dispute period. You need those bureaus open so that furnishers can update your file when disputes are resolved in your favor. Freeze every other bureau first. Once your Big Three disputes are complete, freeze those too.

PHASE TWO: PULL AND MAP EVERY FILE

Once you have frozen the secondary bureaus, pull your complete credit picture. That means all three reports from the Big Three, plus reports from the major secondary bureaus. A complete list is provided in Appendix A of this book.

You are looking for:

- Accounts that do not belong to you (mixed files, identity errors)
- Duplicate accounts listed more than once
- Outdated information that should have aged off (most negatives must be removed after seven years)
- Incorrect balances, limits, payment histories, or statuses
- Accounts in collections that are past the statute of limitations
- Discharged debts that are still showing as owed
- Incorrect personal information (wrong name spelling, wrong address, wrong Social Security Number[SSN])

Create a master log. List every negative item, which bureau it appears on, the creditor name, account number, date of first delinquency, and the specific error. This log is your battle plan.

PHASE THREE: DISPUTE, VERIFY, AND REMOVE

Now you dispute. For every item on your master log, you send a dispute letter to the bureau that carries the error. The bureau then contacts the original furnisher (the creditor or collection agency) and asks them to verify the information.

Here is the key: furnishers have thirty days to respond to a dispute. Many of them do not respond at all, or respond with incomplete information. When they fail to fully verify the item, the bureau must delete it.

This is not a loophole. This is federal law. The Fair Credit Reporting Act (FCRA) requires every item to be verifiable. If it is not verifiable, it cannot remain on your report.

The dispute process is covered in full detail in Part Six. For now, know the core truth: the more items you dispute, the more items will be removed because the verification system is imperfect and many furnishers cannot meet the legal standard of verification.

THE FREEZE STRATEGY IN PRACTICE

After your disputes are complete and the dust settles, you freeze the Big Three as well. At that point, your file is clean, locked, and protected. You have a credit score based only on accurate, verifiable information.

From there, Part Seven of this book covers how to rebuild positive credit on top of that clean foundation.

The Credit Repair System: Freeze everything you can. Pull every report. Dispute everything that cannot be verified. Remove what is not provable. Rebuild on the clean foundation.

Chapter 2

Your Credit Score: What it is and What it is Not

Before you can fix your credit, you need to understand what a credit score actually is. Most people have a vague idea but not the full picture.

THE BASICS

A credit score is a three-digit number, typically between 300 and 850, generated by a mathematical model that analyzes the information in your credit report. The score predicts the statistical likelihood that you will be more than ninety days late on a payment in the next twenty-four months.

That is all it is: a prediction. It is not a measure of your character, your intelligence, your income, or your net worth. It is a number calculated from the data in your file at one moment in time.

SCORE RANGES

Different lenders use different thresholds, but here is a general guide:

- 800–850: Exceptional. You qualify for the best rates on anything.
- 740–799: Very Good. You qualify for most products at strong rates.
- 670–739: Good. Most lenders will approve you. Rates are competitive.
- 580–669: Fair. You can get credit but expect higher rates and stricter terms.

- 300–579: Poor. Most traditional lenders will decline. You need a repair strategy.

WHAT ACTUALLY AFFECTS YOUR SCORE

FICO, the dominant scoring model used to assess your creditworthiness, weights the following factors:

1. Payment history (35 percent). This is the biggest factor. Late payments, defaults, and collections hurt you most here.
2. Amounts owed (30 percent). This is your credit utilization. How much of your available credit are you using? Under 30 percent is the standard target. Under 10 percent is ideal.
3. Length of credit history (15 percent). Having older accounts can help, whereas closing old accounts can hurt.
4. Credit mix (10 percent). Having a mix of credit types strengthens your score. The ideal mix includes revolving credit (credit cards), installment loans (auto loans, personal loans, etc.), and a mortgage if applicable. Car loans are among the easiest installment accounts to obtain and are one of the fastest ways to add a positive installment tradeline to a thin file.
5. New credit (10 percent). Hard inquiries from recent applications temporarily lower your score.

Notice what is not on that list: your income, your job history, your bank account balance, and your assets. A high earner with terrible payment habits will have a lower score than a modest earner who pays every bill on time.

THE TWO TYPES OF INQUIRIES

A hard inquiry happens when a lender pulls your credit to make a lending decision. It can lower your score by a few points for up to twelve months. Multiple hard inquiries for the same type of loan (auto loan, mortgage, etc.) within a short window are usually counted as one inquiry.

A soft inquiry happens when you check your own credit, when employers run background checks, or when you get pre-approved offers. Soft inquiries do not affect your score.

SCORES ARE NOT UNIVERSAL

It is critical to understand that there is no single credit score. FICO alone has over twenty versions currently in active use. VantageScore, the main competitor, has its own versions. Different lenders also use different models and different versions. Your mortgage lender may be looking at a completely different score than your auto lender.

When you check your score through a free service, you are often seeing a generic educational score, not the actual score a specific lender will use. This is not fraud. It is just the reality of a fragmented scoring market.

Part Five of this book covers scoring models in depth. For now, the key takeaway is this: fixing the underlying data in your credit report improves all of your scores across all models because they all draw from the same raw data.

Part Two

Understanding the Credit Bureau System

Chapter 3

The Big Three: Equifax, Experian, and TransUnion

The three major credit bureaus are not government agencies. They are private, for-profit corporations. They collect data about you, package it, and sell it to anyone with a permissible purpose under the law. Understanding what they are and how they make money is essential to understanding how to deal with them.

CORPORATE PROFILES

Equifax

Equifax is headquartered in Atlanta, Georgia. It is the oldest of the three major bureaus, founded in 1899 as the Retail Credit Company. It went public on the New York Stock Exchange. Equifax operates in twenty-four countries and generates over five billion dollars in annual revenue.

In 2017, Equifax suffered the most damaging data breach in consumer credit history. Hackers accessed the personal information of approximately 147 million Americans, including SSNs, birth dates, home addresses, and in some cases, driver's license numbers and credit card data. Equifax paid approximately 575 million dollars in settlements with the Federal Trade Commission (FTC) and CFPB. No leadership faced criminal charges.

If you were an adult American in 2017, your data is almost certainly in the hands of third parties as a result of this breach.

Experian

Experian is headquartered in Dublin, Ireland, with major North American operations in Costa Mesa, California. It is the largest credit bureau in the world by revenue, generating over six billion dollars annually. Experian operates in over forty countries.

In the United States, Experian has been the most aggressive bureau in marketing credit monitoring products directly to consumers, often running online ads that look like free credit report services but lead to subscription services. Read the fine print on anything Experian offers.

TransUnion

TransUnion is headquartered in Chicago, Illinois. It went public in 2015 and generates approximately four billion dollars annually. TransUnion has expanded heavily into emerging markets in recent years.

TransUnion is generally regarded as more consumer-friendly than the other two in terms of its dispute process, but that is a relative comparison.

HOW THE BIG THREE MAKE MONEY

Understanding the revenue model explains everything about why the bureaus behave the way they do.

The bureaus make money in four primary ways:

1. Selling credit reports to lenders, landlords, employers, and others with permissible purposes.
2. Selling credit scores and analytical products to lenders.
3. Selling marketing data, including prescreened lists of consumers who meet certain criteria.
4. Selling consumer-facing products like credit monitoring subscriptions, identity theft protection, and score simulators.

Notice who their primary customers are: **not you**. Their primary customers are the businesses that pay for bulk access to credit data. You are the product, not the customer. This is why their dispute resolution systems are designed to be difficult. Every dispute that results in a deletion reduces the value of the data they sell.

THE METRO 2 FORMAT

When a creditor reports information to the bureaus, they use a standardized format called Metro 2. This is a data transmission format that specifies exactly how to report account information, including account type codes, payment status codes, balance information, credit limit information, and date fields including the critically important Date of First Delinquency.

The Date of First Delinquency is the date when you first fell behind on a payment that eventually led to a default. This date is critical because it starts the seven-year clock for how long a negative item can legally remain on your report. If a collector or bureau has this date wrong, you have grounds for dispute and potentially litigation.

WHERE THE BIG THREE GET THEIR DATA

The three bureaus do not generate information. They collect it from a network of data furnishers that report account information on a monthly basis. Understanding who reports to whom helps you understand where errors originate and where to direct your disputes.

Entities that report to all three major bureaus:

- National banks and regional banks (checking, savings, and credit accounts).
- Credit unions.
- Major credit card issuers (Visa, Mastercard, American Express, and Discover).
- Auto lenders and auto finance companies.

- Mortgage servicers and mortgage originators.
- Federal and private student loan servicers.
- National retail chains with store credit cards (Target, Nordstrom, Home Depot, etc.).
- Major collection agencies and debt buyers.

Entities that report to some but not all bureaus:

- Smaller regional banks and community banks may report to only one or two bureaus.
- Some landlords and property management companies now report rent payments to select bureaus.
- Utility companies and telecom providers generally do not report to the Big Three directly but may report to the National Consumer Telecom and Utilities Exchange (NCTUE), covered in Part Four.
- Fintech lenders and buy-now-pay-later providers vary widely. Some report to all three. Others report to only one or none. Check the terms before using any fintech credit product.

Public records sources (courts, county recorders, etc.) once fed bankruptcies, judgments, and tax liens into credit files. Civil judgments and tax liens were largely removed from the Big Three files in 2017 and 2018 due to data quality problems. Bankruptcies are still reported through public records and remain the primary public record category in modern credit files.

HOW TO FREEZE YOUR CREDIT: STEP-BY-STEP

Placing a security freeze at all three major bureaus is free and permanent until you lift it, and is one of the most powerful protective tools available to you. Here is the exact process for each bureau:

Equifax Freeze

1. Go to www.equifax.com/personal/credit-report-services/

2. Click "Place or Manage a Security Freeze"
3. Create a myEquifax account if you do not already have one. (You will need your SSN, date of birth, and current address)
4. Follow the prompts to place the freeze. You will receive a confirmation and a PIN. Save the PIN.
5. Phone option: 1-800-349-9960
6. Mail option: Equifax Security Freeze, P.O. Box 105788, Atlanta, GA 30348

Experian Freeze

1. Go to www.experian.com/freeze/center.html
2. Click "Add a security freeze"
3. Create a free Experian account if you do not have one.
4. Provide your personal information to verify your identity.
5. Submit the freeze request. You will receive email confirmation.
6. Phone option: 1-888-397-3742
7. Mail option: Experian Security Freeze, P.O. Box 9554, Allen, TX 75013

TransUnion Freeze

1. Go to www.transunion.com/credit-freeze
2. Click "Add a Credit Freeze"
3. Create a myTransUnion account.
4. Complete identity verification.
5. Place the freeze and save your confirmation PIN.
6. Phone option: 1-888-909-8872
7. Mail option: TransUnion LLC, P.O. Box 160, Woodlyn, PA 19094

Freeze all three bureaus. It is free. It takes about fifteen minutes total. It does not hurt your score. When you need to apply for credit, you temporarily lift the freeze at the specific bureau the lender uses, then refreeze after. Lenders will tell you which bureau they pull.

HOW ERRORS ENTER YOUR FILE

Bureau files are not curated. They are largely automated data intake systems. Errors enter in several ways:

- Furnisher errors: The original creditor or collector submits incorrect data through the Metro 2 system. This includes wrong balances, wrong payment histories, wrong dates.
- Mixed files: The bureau matches data from one consumer to another consumer's file because of similar names, SSN errors, or address overlap. This is extremely common and extremely damaging.
- Re-aging: A collector buys an old debt and reports it with a new, more recent delinquency date to make it appear newer and keep it on your report longer. **This is illegal**.
- Duplicate reporting: The same debt appears multiple times, once from the original creditor and again from one or more collection agencies.
- Failure to update: A creditor settles a debt or receives payment but never updates the bureau with the correct status.

Studies consistently find that approximately one in five credit reports contains an error significant enough to result in credit denial. You should assume your report has errors until you verify otherwise.

Chapter 4

How Credit Bureaus Build Your File

Your credit file is built from a combination of data you generate (credit applications, account activity, etc.) and data reported about you (payment history, delinquencies, public records, etc.). Understanding how this data flows in and how the bureaus process it helps you identify and attack errors more effectively.

CREDIT HEADERS

The header of your credit file contains your identifying information: legal name, any known name variations, current and previous addresses, date of birth, SSN, and phone numbers. This data is derived from credit applications you have submitted over the years and from public records.

Header errors are more common than people realize. If your name is misspelled, your date of birth is wrong, or there is a wrong SSN associated with your file, it can cause serious problems including mixed files (where someone else's data appears in your report) and split files (where your data is scattered across multiple incomplete files).

When you pull your credit reports, check the header section first. Dispute any inaccuracy in your personal information before disputing tradelines.

TRADELINES

A tradeline is any account that appears in your credit file. This includes credit cards, auto loans, student loans, mortgages, personal loans, retail accounts, and collection accounts. Each tradeline contains a detailed history of the account including:

- The creditor name and account number.
- The type of account.
- The date the account was opened.
- The credit limit or original loan amount.
- The current balance.
- The payment history, typically as a rolling 24-month grid showing on-time or late payments.
- The current account status (open, closed, charged off, in collections, or paid).
- The Date of First Delinquency, if applicable.

PUBLIC RECORDS

Prior to 2017, credit reports included civil judgments and tax liens as public records. The Big Three removed almost all civil judgments and tax liens from credit reports in 2017 and 2018 because the data quality was so poor. Most of what remained was inaccurate.

The one public record category still commonly appearing on credit reports is bankruptcy. Chapter 7 bankruptcy stays on your report for ten years from the filing date. Chapter 13 bankruptcy stays for seven years from the filing date.

INQUIRIES

Your report also contains a section listing inquiries. Hard inquiries from lenders stay on your report for two years but only affect your score for twelve months. If you see hard inquiries you do not recognize, dispute them. Unauthorized hard inquiries are a possible sign of fraud and are a legitimate dispute target.

THE SEVEN-YEAR CLOCK

Under the FCRA, most negative information must be removed from your credit report after seven years from the Date of First Delinquency. This includes:

- Late payments
- Charge-offs
- Collections
- Civil judgments (now largely excluded anyway)
- Tax liens (now largely excluded)

Bankruptcies have their own timeframes: ten years for Chapter 7, seven years for Chapter 13.

Positive information can stay on your report indefinitely. Paid accounts with perfect histories are valuable and can remain.

The seven-year clock starts from the Date of First Delinquency on the original account, not from the date a collection agency buys the debt. Collectors frequently try to re-age debt by reporting a newer first delinquency date. If you see this happening, it is a violation of the FCRA and the Fair Debt Collection Practices Act.

Chapter 5

The Reporting Cycle and Timing Your Strategy

Credit reports are not updated in real time. They are updated in cycles, and understanding those cycles helps you time your strategy for maximum impact.

THE MONTHLY REPORTING CYCLE

Most creditors report to the bureaus once a month. Each creditor has a specific reporting date, which is often the statement close date for credit cards. The bureau receives the update and incorporates it within a day or two.

This means your credit report and score can change significantly from one day to the next based purely on timing. A credit card balance that posts two days before the reporting date will show on your report. The same balance paid two days before reporting would not.

When you are preparing to apply for a major loan, pay down credit card balances before the statement close date, not the payment due date. The balance that posts to your credit report is the balance at statement close.

DISPUTE RESOLUTION TIMING

The FCRA requires bureaus to complete their investigation of your dispute within thirty days. In practice, many investigations are resolved faster. But the thirty-day window is important to know because:

- If the bureau does not complete the investigation within thirty days, they must delete the item.
- If you submit additional information after the initial dispute, the bureau may get up to fifteen more days.
- The thirty-day clock does not start until the bureau receives your dispute.

Send all disputes by certified mail with a return receipt requested. This gives you a paper trail showing exactly when the bureau received your dispute. If you dispute online, screenshot everything including a timestamp.

WHEN TO PULL YOUR REPORTS

Pull all three reports at the start of your credit repair process. Do not space them out. You want a complete picture at the same moment in time because the same account can appear differently on different bureau files.

After you send disputes, wait thirty-five days before pulling your reports to check results. This gives the bureau time to complete their investigation and for the updated file to be reflected.

THE ANNUAL FREE REPORT

Under federal law, every consumer is entitled to one free credit report from each of the Big Three every twelve months. The official source is www.AnnualCreditReport.com, which is the only federally mandated free source. Do not use any other site claiming to offer free reports without reading the terms carefully.

During the COVID-19 pandemic, the bureaus expanded access to weekly free reports. As of this writing, weekly free reports remain available through www.AnnualCreditReport.com. Pull them. Use them.

Your Right to Free Credit Reports

You are also entitled to a free credit report any time one of the following occurs:

- A lender, landlord, employer, or insurer denies you credit, housing, employment, or insurance based on your credit report. You have sixty days from the adverse action notice to request the specific report that was used.
- You are unemployed and plan to seek employment within sixty days.
- You are on public assistance.
- You believe your file contains inaccurate information due to fraud or identity theft.

THE SUBSCRIPTION TRAP: WHAT YOU DO NOT NEED TO PAY FOR

The credit bureaus are extraordinarily aggressive in selling subscription services for credit monitoring. When you visit their websites, request a report, or set up a dispute account, you will be pushed toward paid products ranging from ten to forty dollars per month. You do not need to pay for any of them.

Every major bureau allows you to create a free account and log in to see your reports and basic score information without paying for a subscription.

The free accounts are:

- Equifax: Create a myEquifax account at equifax.com. Free access to your Equifax report and basic score.
- Experian: Create a free account at experian.com. Free access to your Experian report and FICO Score 8.
- TransUnion: Create a free account at transunion.com. Free access to your TransUnion report.

Beyond the bureau free accounts, most financial products you already have provide free credit monitoring at no charge:

- Many major credit cards (Chase, Capital One, Citi, Discover, American Express) provide a free FICO or VantageScore in your account dashboard, updated monthly.
- Most banks and credit unions provide free credit score access through their mobile apps.
- Personal finance apps including Credit Karma, Credit Sesame, and Mint provide free VantageScores with no paid requirement.

The monitoring services the bureaus sell are not required for credit repair. Cancel any you are currently paying for unless you have a specific reason to maintain them.

FINDING LENDERS THAT USE SOFT PULLS FIRST

As discussed earlier, a hard inquiry occurs when a lender pulls your credit to make a lending decision. It can reduce your score by a few points. A soft inquiry is a preliminary check that does not affect your score at all.

Many lenders offer pre-qualification tools that use only a soft pull, allowing you to see likely approval odds and estimated rates before committing to a formal application. Use these first. Only submit a formal application when pre-qualification indicates a strong likelihood of approval.

Lenders with widely available soft-pull pre-qualification tools include:

- American Express: Pre-qualification tool at www.americanexpress.com shows cards you are likely to be approved for with no impact to your score.
- Capital One: Pre-approval tool at www.capitalone.com uses a soft pull for personal and business cards.
- Discover: Pre-qualification at www.discover.com for most card products.

- Citibank: Pre-qualification available at www.citibank.com for selected products.
- Credit Karma Marketplace: Matches you with financial products using soft pulls across multiple lenders simultaneously.
- Most mortgage lenders offer a soft-pull pre-qualification conversation before any formal application. Ask specifically before allowing any credit pull.

When contacting any lender, ask this question before providing your SSN: "Will this inquiry be a hard pull or a soft pull?" If they cannot answer, do not proceed until they can. Hard inquiries are permanently on your report for two years. Protect them.

Part Three

The Law is on Your Side

Chapter 6

The Fair Credit Reporting Act: Your Primary Weapon

The Fair Credit Reporting Act, known as the FCRA, is the federal law that governs credit reporting in the United States. It was originally passed in 1970 and has been amended several times since. It is the legal foundation for every strategy in this book.

You do not need to memorize the FCRA. You need to understand the key rights it gives you and how to use them.

YOUR CORE RIGHTS UNDER THE FCRA

The Right to Access Your File

You have the right to know what is in your credit file. The bureaus must provide you with a copy of your report upon request. You are entitled to a free report from each major bureau every twelve months.

You are also entitled to a free report if:

- You were denied credit, employment, housing, or insurance based on your credit report (within sixty days of the adverse action notice).
- You are a victim of identity theft and have placed a fraud alert.
- You are on public assistance.
- You are unemployed and plan to apply for work within sixty days.

The Right to Dispute Inaccurate Information

This is the cornerstone right. The FCRA requires that credit report information be accurate, complete, and up to date. If it is not, you have the right to dispute it.

When you submit a dispute, the bureau must:

1. Notify the furnisher of the dispute within five business days.
2. Conduct a reasonable reinvestigation.
3. Complete the investigation within thirty days (forty-five days if you provide additional information).
4. Correct or delete inaccurate, incomplete, or unverifiable information.
5. Notify you of the results.

The Right to Have Outdated Information Removed

Most negative items must be removed after seven years. The bureaus are required to maintain systems that automatically suppress outdated information, but errors do happen. You can dispute outdated items and demand their removal.

The Right to Know Who Pulled Your File

You have the right to see a list of everyone who has accessed your credit report in the past two years (five years if for employment purposes). This lets you identify unauthorized inquiries.

The Right to Place a Fraud Alert

If you believe you are a victim of identity theft, you can place a fraud alert on your file with one bureau, and that bureau must notify the others. A fraud alert requires lenders to take extra steps to verify your identity before opening new credit in your name.

The Right to Place a Security Freeze

A security freeze (also called a credit freeze) prevents new creditors from accessing your file altogether. Since September 2018, placing and lifting a credit freeze is free with all three major bureaus and at most specialty bureaus. This is one of the most powerful tools available to you.

WHAT THE FCRA REQUIRES OF FURNISHERS

Furnishers are the companies that report data to the bureaus: banks, credit card companies, auto lenders, student loan servicers, and collection agencies.

The FCRA has specific requirements for furnishers:

- They must report accurate information.
- They must have procedures to prevent reporting information they know is inaccurate.
- When they receive notification of a dispute from a bureau, they must investigate and respond accurately.
- If they find that information they reported is inaccurate, they must correct it or delete it.

Furnisher violations are a major source of FCRA litigation. If a furnisher continues to report inaccurate information after being notified of a dispute and failing to correct it, they may be liable for actual damages, statutory damages, and attorney's fees. This is why involving an attorney can be valuable in serious cases.

THE RIGHT TO SUE

The FCRA gives you the right to sue bureaus and furnishers in federal court for violations. If you win, you can recover:

- Actual damages (any financial harm the violation caused).
- Statutory damages of $100 to $1,000 per willful violation, even without proving actual harm.
- Punitive damages for willful violations.
- Attorney's fees and court costs.

This is not theoretical. Thousands of FCRA lawsuits are filed every year. Many consumers win significant settlements without ever going to trial because the cost of defending an FCRA case often exceeds the cost of settlement. An FCRA attorney typically works on contingency, meaning you pay nothing upfront.

Chapter 7

The CFPB: The Bureau That Watches the Bureaus

The Consumer Financial Protection Bureau, known as the CFPB, was created by the Dodd-Frank Wall Street Reform and Consumer Protection Act of 2010. It is a federal agency with supervisory and enforcement authority over the credit reporting industry. Understanding the CFPB is essential because it is one of your most powerful escalation tools.

WHAT THE CFPB DOES

The CFPB supervises the Big Three credit reporting agencies. It can examine their records, require documents, conduct interviews, and issue enforcement orders. It has the authority to impose civil money penalties for violations of federal consumer financial law.

The CFPB also accepts consumer complaints and has received millions of complaints about credit reporting since its creation. In recent years, credit or consumer reporting has consistently been the top complaint category at the CFPB.

HOW TO FILE A CFPB COMPLAINT

Filing a CFPB complaint is free, straightforward, and has real teeth. Here is the process:

1. Go to www.consumerfinance.gov/complaint
2. Select "Credit reporting, credit repair services, or other personal consumer reports"
3. Select the specific issue (inaccurate information, improper use of your report, problem with a company's investigation, etc.).

4. Select the company you are complaining about.
5. Describe your issue in detail. Include dates, account numbers, and a clear description of what happened and what the bureau or furnisher failed to do.
6. Upload any supporting documents (dispute letters, bureau responses, evidence of the error, etc.).
7. Submit.

The CFPB will forward your complaint to the company, which typically has fifteen days to respond. The CFPB then publishes complaint data publicly, which creates reputational pressure. Companies that accumulate large numbers of unresolved complaints draw regulatory attention.

More importantly: CFPB complaints frequently result in faster dispute resolution. When a bureau receives a complaint that has been formally filed with a federal regulator, the urgency of resolution increases significantly compared to a standard dispute letter.

CFPB ENFORCEMENT ACTIONS

The CFPB has pursued significant enforcement actions against all three major bureaus.

Some highlights:

- In 2017, the CFPB fined Equifax, Experian, and TransUnion a combined $23.7 million for deceptive marketing of credit monitoring products and for failing to provide consumers with the free annual reports they were entitled to.
- In 2023, the CFPB sued Experian, alleging that Experian conducted sham investigations of consumer disputes and failed to maintain reasonable procedures to ensure maximum possible accuracy. The CFPB alleged Experian simply rubber-stamped data reported by furnishers without any genuine investigation.

- In 2024, the CFPB ordered Equifax to pay $15 million for failing to properly investigate consumer disputes.

These enforcement actions are significant for two reasons. First, they validate what consumers have long known: the bureau's dispute processes are often inadequate. Second, they establish regulatory precedent that you can reference in your own disputes and correspondence.

STATE ATTORNEYS GENERAL

State attorneys general have concurrent authority to enforce the FCRA in their states. Several states, including California, New York, and Illinois, have enacted credit reporting laws that go beyond the federal FCRA. If you live in one of these states, you may have additional protections.

Filing a complaint with your state attorney general (AG) is another escalation tool. State AGs take consumer credit complaints seriously and often coordinate with the CFPB.

Chapter 8

Other Laws That Protect You

The FCRA is your primary weapon, but there are several other federal and state laws that work alongside it. A complete credit repair strategy knows all of them.

THE FAIR DEBT COLLECTION PRACTICES ACT (FDCPA)

The FDCPA prohibits abusive, deceptive, and unfair debt collection practices by third-party debt collectors. It does not apply to original creditors collecting their own debts, only to third-party collectors.

Key FDCPA rights:

- Debt collectors cannot call before 8 a.m. or after 9 p.m.
- Debt collectors cannot contact you at work if you tell them your employer prohibits such calls.
- Debt collectors cannot use abusive or threatening language.
- If you send a written cease-and-desist letter, the collector must stop contacting you (though they can still pursue legal action).
- Debt collectors must send you a written validation notice within five days of first contact, telling you the amount of the debt, the name of the original creditor, and your right to dispute.
- If you dispute the debt in writing within thirty days of the validation notice, the collector must stop collection activity until they verify the debt.

FDCPA violations can result in statutory damages of up to $1,000 per lawsuit, plus actual damages and attorney's fees. Many FDCPA attorneys work on contingency.

THE CREDIT REPAIR ORGANIZATIONS ACT (CROA)

The Credit Repair Organizations Act is the federal law that governs credit repair companies. It was passed in 1996.

Key provisions:

- Credit repair companies cannot charge upfront fees before services are fully performed.
- Contracts must be in writing with specific disclosures.
- You have three days to cancel a contract with a credit repair company.
- Credit repair companies cannot advise you to make false statements or mislead bureaus or creditors.

The Credit Services Acts at the state level, which I was personally involved in pioneering with the California Credit Services Act of 1984, provide additional protections that vary by state. Most states now have some version of this law.

THE EQUAL CREDIT OPPORTUNITY ACT (ECOA)

The ECOA prohibits credit discrimination based on race, color, religion, national origin, sex, marital status, age, or because you receive public assistance. When a lender denies you credit, they must give you a specific reason.

If you are denied credit, you have the right to request the specific reasons for denial. Those reasons help you identify exactly which items on your credit report caused the problem and prioritize your dispute strategy.

STATE-LEVEL CREDIT LAWS

Several states have enacted credit reporting and consumer protection laws that exceed federal protections.

Notable examples:

- California has the California Consumer Credit Reporting Agencies Act and the California Consumer Privacy Act (CCPA), which gives consumers broad rights over their personal data held by data brokers and other companies.
- New York has limitations on using credit reports in employment decisions and prohibits reporting certain types of debt.
- Illinois has restrictions on credit checks in employment.

Know the laws of your state. If you are in California, you have more rights than the federal floor. Do not leave them unused.

Part Four

Secondary and Specialty Bureaus

Chapter 9

Beyond the Big Three: The Full Credit Ecosystem

This is where most credit repair strategies fail. People spend all their time on Equifax, Experian, and TransUnion and ignore the dozens of other agencies that hold data on them. Then they wonder why they still cannot get approved for an apartment, a checking account, or a telecom plan even after cleaning up their Big Three files.

Here is the reality: there are over forty specialty consumer reporting agencies in the United States that collect and sell information about consumers. You have the right to your file from every single one of them, and you have the right to dispute inaccuracies in every single one of them.

WHY SECONDARY BUREAUS MATTER

Different industries use different reporting agencies:

- Landlords frequently use CoreLogic Rental Property Solutions, CLEAR from TransUnion, or specialty tenant screening agencies.
- Banks use ChexSystems or Early Warning Services to screen new checking account applications. A negative ChexSystems record can prevent you from opening a bank account for five years.
- Insurance companies use LexisNexis Risk Solutions and other data sources to build insurance risk profiles.
- Telecommunications companies use National Consumer Telecom and Utilities Exchange (NCTUE) data.
- Employers often use LexisNexis or similar products for background and identity screening.

- Auto dealerships and lenders may use specialty auto credit files.

If you are being denied for services you cannot explain with your Big Three files, the answer is often in a specialty bureau file you do not know about. The Credit Repair System addresses all of them.

THE MAJOR SECONDARY BUREAUS

Innovis

Innovis is sometimes called the fourth major bureau. It operates similarly to the Big Three and has files on millions of Americans. Many creditors report to Innovis. You can request your free Innovis file and place a freeze through their website or by calling them directly.

Contact: www.innovis.com or 1-800-540-2505.

LexisNexis Risk Solutions

LexisNexis holds a massive amount of data on consumers, including public records, property records, court records, license data, and more. It is used by insurance companies, employers, banks, and lenders. Many people have no idea LexisNexis has a file on them.

You can request your LexisNexis consumer disclosure report at www.risk.lexisnexis.com/consumerdisclosure. You can also place a security freeze at LexisNexis.

SageStream/ID Analytics

SageStream (now operating under the LexisNexis brand in some capacities) is used primarily by financial services companies and telecom providers. It uses alternative data for credit scoring.

CoreLogic

CoreLogic holds massive amounts of real estate and property data. Its subsidiary, CoreLogic Rental Property Solutions, provides tenant screening services. If you have ever been evicted or had rental payment issues, CoreLogic likely has a record of it.

Request your CoreLogic consumer file through their website or by mail.

MicroBilt/PRBC

MicroBilt serves non-traditional lenders including payday lenders, rent-to-own companies, and subprime financial services. PRBC (Pay Rent Build Credit) allows consumers to report rent and utility payments to build credit with non-traditional lenders. You have the right to your MicroBilt file.

NCTUE

The National Consumer Telecom and Utilities Exchange collects data from telecommunications companies including AT&T, T-Mobile, and others, along with utilities. If you have unpaid phone or utility bills, they may appear here and affect your ability to open new accounts. You can request your NCTUE file through www.equifax.com, as Equifax manages this exchange.

BANKING-SPECIFIC REPORTING AGENCIES

ChexSystems

ChexSystems is the most important specialty bureau for banking access. If you have had a checking account closed for negative reasons including overdrafts, returned checks, or fraud, ChexSystems likely has a record. Most banks check ChexSystems before opening a new account for you.

A negative ChexSystems record can stay for five years. The FCRA applies to ChexSystems, which means you have the right to your file, the right to dispute inaccuracies, and the right to seek removal of unverifiable items.

Request your free ChexSystems report at www.chexsystems.com. You can also request it by mail.

Early Warning Services

Early Warning Services is owned jointly by several major banks including Bank of America, Chase, Wells Fargo, US Bank, and Capital One. It operates the Zelle payment network as well as a banking screening database, and it functions similarly to ChexSystems.

If major banks are closing your applications, Early Warning Services may be the reason. Request your file at earlywarning.com.

THE FREEZE-EVERYTHING STRATEGY APPLIED

Here is the complete list of agencies where you should request your file and place a freeze, sorted by priority:

1. ChexSystems (chexsystems.com)—critical if you need a bank account
2. Early Warning Services (earlywarning.com)—critical if applying to major banks
3. LexisNexis (risk.lexisnexis.com / consumerdisclosure)—critical for insurance and employment
4. CoreLogic (corelogic.com)—critical if applying for rental housing
5. Innovis (innovis.com)—general credit, treated like a fourth major bureau
6. NCTUE (via equifax.com)—critical for telecom services
7. MicroBilt (microbilt.com)—if using subprime or alternative lenders
8. SageStream—request via LexisNexis consumer disclosure process

Appendix A of this book provides the contact information, freeze request process, and dispute process for each of these agencies. Do not skip this step.

Part Five

Credit Scores Explained

Chapter 10

FICO, VantageScore, and the Scoring Wars

The credit scoring market has become a battlefield in recent years. For decades, FICO held a virtual monopoly on credit scores used in lending decisions. That monopoly is eroding, but FICO is still dominant. Understanding the landscape helps you understand what matters for each type of loan.

FICO: STILL THE KING

FICO scores are used in over ninety percent of lending decisions in the United States. FICO has multiple score versions currently in active use:

- FICO Score 2, 4, and 5: These are the classic versions still required for mortgage underwriting under Fannie Mae and Freddie Mac guidelines. Each version is used with a specific bureau (FICO 2 with Experian, FICO 4 with TransUnion, FICO 5 with Equifax).
- FICO Score 8: The most widely used version for credit card and auto loan decisions. Most educational score products that show you "your FICO score" are showing you FICO 8.
- FICO Score 9: An updated model that treats paid collections differently (they have less impact) and ignores medical debt collections. Few lenders have adopted it despite its consumer-friendly changes.
- FICO Score 10 and 10T: The newest versions. FICO 10T uses trended data, meaning it looks at the direction of your balances over time, not just the current snapshot. Consumers who have been paying down debt score better. Adoption by lenders is growing slowly.

VANTAGESCORE: THE CHALLENGER

VantageScore was created jointly by the three major bureaus in 2006 as a competitor to FICO. Its main version in use today is VantageScore 4.0.

Key differences from FICO:

- VantageScore can generate a score with as little as one month of credit history. FICO requires at least six months.
- VantageScore 4.0 incorporates trending data (similar to FICO 10T).
- VantageScore treats multiple student loan inquiries and medical debt differently from FICO.

In 2023, the Federal Housing Finance Agency (FHFA), which regulates Fannie Mae and Freddie Mac, approved both Classic FICO and VantageScore 4.0 for conventional mortgage underwriting. This was a major shift. For the first time, the two largest mortgage buyers in the country will accept a non-FICO score for conventional loans.

This matters for credit repair because VantageScore 4.0 scores some consumers higher than classic FICO, particularly those with shorter histories or thin files. If you have been told you do not have enough credit history to qualify for a mortgage, check your VantageScore.

WHAT SCORE DOES MY LENDER USE?

The honest answer is: you do not know until you ask. Here is a practical guide:

- Mortgage lenders: Classic FICO (version 2, 4, or 5) for conforming loans. They pull all three bureaus and typically use the middle score. VantageScore 4.0 is being phased in.
- Auto lenders: FICO Auto Score 2, 4, 5, or 8 are common. Some use generic FICO 8.

- Credit card issuers: Usually FICO 8 or a proprietary model derived from bureau data.
- Personal loans and fintech lenders: Often use FICO 8, VantageScore, or a proprietary model.
- Landlords and tenant screeners: Often use VantageScore or a specialty rental score.

ALTERNATIVE DATA AND NEW SCORING MODELS

The credit scoring world is expanding to incorporate data that traditional models ignored:

- Rent payment data: Platforms like RentTrack, Rental Kharma, and credit bureau products allow rent payments to be reported and scored. This can significantly help consumers who have been paying rent on time for years but have thin traditional credit files.
- Utility and telecom data: The NCTUE data described in Chapter 9 can feed into scores for consumers with thin files.
- Bank account cash flow data: Open banking models like Fannie Mae Day 1 Certainty use bank account data to verify income and can supplement or substitute for traditional credit data in some underwriting systems.

These alternative data sources are most valuable for consumers in two categories: those with no or thin credit files who have been financially responsible but just never used traditional credit, and those rebuilding from damaged credit who now have positive payment history in non-traditional credit relationships.

Part Six

Advanced Dispute Strategies

Chapter 11

The Complete Dispute System

Most people who try to dispute their credit reports do it wrong. They send a vague letter saying "this is not mine" or "please investigate." The bureau runs it through their automated verification system, the furnisher sends back a generic confirmation, and the item stays.

Effective disputing requires specificity, documentation, and a clear escalation path. Here is the complete system.

STEP ONE: CATEGORIZE YOUR DISPUTES

Not all disputes are the same. Before you write a single letter, categorize every item you are disputing:

1. Identity errors: Wrong name, wrong SSN, wrong address, or wrong date of birth. These are the highest priority because they often indicate mixed files.
2. Account ownership errors: Accounts that do not belong to you at all.
3. Account status errors: Accounts showing as open that are closed, charged off when paid, or in collections when settled.
4. Balance or limit errors: Wrong balances or credit limits that inflate your utilization.
5. Payment history errors: Late payments reported that were not late, missed payments you made.
6. Outdated information: Negative items older than seven years (or ten for Chapter 7 bankruptcy).
7. Re-aged accounts: Items with incorrect Date of First Delinquency that make them appear newer.

Your approach for each category is different. Identity errors require supporting documentation. Account ownership errors require clear denial and request for verification. Outdated items require only the date proof.

STEP TWO: BUILD YOUR EVIDENCE FILE

Before you write dispute letters, gather your evidence:

- Photo ID and Social Security card (for identity verification in your dispute).
- Proof of address (utility bill, bank statement, etc.)
- Payment records for any accounts you are disputing as incorrectly reported.
- Correspondence from original creditors or collection agencies.
- Debt validation letters you received (or did not receive).
- Settlement agreements for any settled accounts.
- Bankruptcy discharge papers if applicable.

Do not attach everything to your first dispute letter. Include only what directly proves the specific error. Save additional documentation for escalation rounds.

STEP THREE: WRITE EFFECTIVE DISPUTE LETTERS

Your dispute letter needs to do six things:

1. Clearly identify you (full legal name, date of birth, last four digits of your SSN, and current address).
2. Clearly identify the item you are disputing (creditor name, account number, which bureau, etc.).
3. State the specific error clearly and factually.
4. State what you are requesting (correction, deletion, or verification).

5. Reference the legal basis if applicable (e.g., "This item is beyond the seven-year reporting period under 15 U.S.C., Section 1681c").
6. Enclose relevant supporting documentation.

What to avoid in dispute letters:

- Do not threaten lawsuits in your first letter. Save legal threats for escalation.
- Do not use form letters downloaded from random websites. Bureaus have seen them all and flag them as "frivolous."
- Do not dispute accurate information. Disputing accurate items is fraud.
- Do not dispute too many items in a single letter. Three to five items per letter per bureau is manageable. More than that risks the letter being flagged as a credit repair mill submission.

STEP FOUR: SEND BY CERTIFIED MAIL

Always send disputes to the bureaus by certified mail with a return receipt requested. The green card showing delivery is your evidence that the thirty-day clock has started. Keep everything.

Bureau dispute addresses:

- Equifax: Equifax Information Services LLC, P.O. Box 740256, Atlanta, GA 30374
- Experian: Experian, P.O. Box 4500, Allen, TX 75013
- TransUnion: TransUnion Consumer Solutions, P.O. Box 2000, Chester, PA 19016

STEP FIVE: REVIEW THE RESULTS

Within thirty-five days of mailing your dispute, you should receive results from the bureau. The bureau will send you one of three responses:

- The item was deleted.
- The item was modified (corrected).
- The item was verified and will remain as is.

If the item was verified and remains, you are not done. You move to Step Six.

STEP SIX: ESCALATION

When a dispute comes back verified but you believe the item is still inaccurate, you escalate. The escalation path is:

1. Send a dispute directly to the furnisher. Under the FCRA, you can dispute with furnishers directly. Send a detailed dispute to the credit card company, collection agency, or original creditor with your evidence. They have thirty days to investigate and correct.
2. File a CFPB complaint. File a formal complaint naming the bureau and the furnisher. Include copies of your dispute letters, the bureau's response, and your evidence. CFPB complaints get attention that dispute letters do not.
3. File a complaint with your state attorney general. Do this simultaneously with the CFPB complaint.
4. Contact an FCRA attorney. If the item has been reinvestigated and remains inaccurate, you may have a viable FCRA claim. Most FCRA attorneys will give a free consultation. If you have a case, they typically work on contingency.

WHAT IS A FRIVOLOUS DISPUTE?

Bureaus are allowed to reject a dispute as frivolous if it has no factual basis or if it is substantially the same dispute the consumer previously submitted. This is a power they abuse.

If a bureau rejects your dispute as frivolous:

- Request the specific basis for the frivolous determination in writing.

- Respond with a more detailed dispute that addresses their stated reason.
- File a CFPB complaint about the frivolous rejection if you believe it was improper.

A dispute is not frivolous just because the bureau verified the item before. A new dispute with new evidence or a different legal basis is a new dispute.

Chapter 12

Dealing with Debt Collectors

Collection accounts are among the most damaging items on a credit report. A single unpaid collection can drop a FICO 8 score by 50–100points. Understanding how to deal with collectors is essential to the repair process.

DEBT VALIDATION: YOUR FIRST MOVE

When a debt collector contacts you for the first time, do not pay anything and do not admit to owning the debt. Your first move is to demand debt validation.

Under the FDCPA, you have thirty days from the collector's first written contact to send a written request for debt validation. Once you send this request, the collector must stop all collection activity until they send you verification of the debt.

Verification means more than just telling you the amount. A proper validation should include:

- The name and address of the original creditor.
- A copy of the original agreement or contract.
- A complete accounting of how the debt balance was calculated, including interest and fees.
- Proof that the collection agency has the legal right to collect (chain of title for purchased debt).

Many collectors cannot provide this. Debt is frequently sold multiple times, and records are often incomplete or lost in the process. When a collector cannot validate, they cannot legally continue collecting, and the account becomes a strong dispute target at the bureaus.

THE STATUTE OF LIMITATIONS

The statute of limitations for debt is separate from the credit reporting period. The statute of limitations is the time a creditor has to sue you to collect a debt. After the statute of limitations expires, the debt is "time-barred," and the collector cannot win a judgment against you in court.

The statute of limitations varies by state and by type of debt, generally ranging from three to ten years. The clock typically starts from the date of your last payment.

Critical warning: If you make a payment, even a small one, on a time-barred debt, you may restart the statute of limitations in some states. Before paying anything on an old debt, know your state's laws.

Time-barred debt can still appear on your credit report until the seven-year reporting period expires. A collector can still try to collect on a time-barred debt (they just cannot sue). But if they threaten to sue on a time-barred debt, that is an FDCPA violation.

PAY FOR DELETE: DOES IT STILL WORK?

Pay for delete is an arrangement where you offer to pay a collection account in full or for a settlement amount in exchange for the collector removing the negative item from your credit report entirely, rather than just updating it to "paid collection."

Pay for delete is not illegal. However, it violates the data accuracy requirements in the Metro 2 reporting agreement most collectors have with the bureaus. Despite this, many collectors agree to it, especially smaller agencies with older debts.

If you want to try pay for delete:

1. Do it in writing before paying anything.

2. Make the agreement contingent on deletion, not just payment.
3. Get the agreement signed by a collector representative.
4. Pay only after the deletion is confirmed on your report.

Under newer FICO scoring models (e.g., FICO 9 or FICO 10), paid collections have significantly less impact on your score than unpaid collections. Under the original FICO 8, which is still the most widely used, a paid collection still hurts almost as much as an unpaid one.

MEDICAL DEBT CHANGES

Medical debt collection reporting has undergone significant changes in recent years:

- As of 2023, Equifax, Experian, and TransUnion no longer include medical collection accounts under $500 on credit reports.
- The three bureaus also removed paid medical collection accounts from reports.
- The CFPB has proposed a rule that would remove all medical debt from credit reports entirely. As of the time of this writing, that rule has not yet been finalized.

If you have medical collections, check your reports. Many of them may already have been removed under the current voluntary bureau policies.

Part Seven

Rebuilding Positive Credit

Chapter 13

Building and Maintaining a Strong Credit Profile

Removing negative items clears the field. Now you build. This chapter covers every strategy for constructing a strong, positive credit profile efficiently.

THE FASTEST LEGAL PATH TO GOOD CREDIT

If you have limited or damaged credit and need to build quickly, this is the sequence:

1. Secured credit card. Open one secured credit card at a bank or credit union. Use it for one small recurring purchase (e.g., streaming service, gas, groceries, etc.). Pay it off in full every month. After twelve months of perfect payment history, request a credit limit increase or an upgrade to an unsecured card.
2. Credit-builder loan. Many credit unions offer credit-builder loans, which are small loans where the loan amount is held in a savings account until the loan is paid off. Every payment is reported to the bureaus. This builds payment history and a loan tradeline simultaneously.
3. Authorized user. Ask a family member or close friend with excellent credit to add you as an authorized user on their oldest, highest-limit credit card. The account history on that card will appear in your credit file, aging your average account age and improving your utilization. You do not even need to use the card.

4. Report your rent. Use a service like RentTrack or ask your property management company if they report to credit bureaus. If they do, every on-time rent payment is building your file.

CREDIT UTILIZATION STRATEGY

Your credit utilization rate, which is the ratio of your total credit card balances to your total credit limits, is the second most important factor in your credit score. Here is how to manage it strategically:

- The standard advice is to stay under 30 percent utilization. That is true but insufficient for an excellent score.
- For the best possible score, stay under 10 percent utilization at the time your statement closes and reports to the bureaus.
- Never let any single card go above 50 percent utilization. Even if your overall utilization is low, a maxed-out individual card hurts you.
- Zero utilization is not the goal. If you have a zero balance on all cards every month, the scoring model has no recent payment data to evaluate. Keep at least one card with a small balance that you pay in full.

WHICH ACCOUNTS TO OPEN AND WHEN

A diversified credit profile scores better than a one-dimensional one. Here is the build sequence:

1. Start with one secured card. One account, perfect payment history.
2. After six months, add a credit-builder loan from a credit union.
3. After twelve months of perfect history, apply for one unsecured card (store cards and gas cards are easiest to start with).

4. After eighteen to twenty-four months, consider a second credit card from a different issuer.
5. Once your score is above 680, you can begin working toward installment credit products.

Do not apply for multiple cards at once. Space applications at least six months apart to minimize hard inquiry impact.

DON'T CLOSE OLD ACCOUNTS

One of the most common mistakes people make is closing credit accounts they no longer use. Closing an account does two negative things:

- It removes the credit limit from your calculation, which increases your utilization rate.
- Once the account ages off your report (usually ten years after closing), it removes the history length from your file.

Keep old accounts open even if you do not use them. Put a small recurring charge on each one every few months so it stays active and does not get closed by the issuer for inactivity.

HOW LONG DOES IT TAKE TO REBUILD?

This is the question everyone asks. The honest answer:

- After removing major negatives: 3–6 months to see significant score improvement as the file recalibrates.
- From 580–680: Typically 12–18 months with disciplined execution of the strategies above.
- From 580–740+: Typically 2–4 years with no new negative events.
- From a fresh bankruptcy: A 700+ score is achievable within 2–3

years with the right rebuild strategy, despite common belief that bankruptcy ruins credit for a decade.

The clock on your credit score starts the moment you take action. Every month you delay is a month added to your rebuild timeline. Start now.

MAINTAINING YOUR CREDIT AFTER THE REBUILD

Credit repair without a maintenance plan is like losing weight without changing eating habits. The work you put into removing negatives and building positive history must be protected by a consistent ongoing practice. Here is the annual maintenance routine.

The Annual Credit Review

- January: Pull all three reports from www.AnnualCreditReport.com. Review every tradeline for errors, new accounts you did not open, and outdated negatives that should have aged off.
- April: Check your score from each bureau through free accounts or your card issuer dashboard. Note the trend. A score that was improving should continue to improve if your file is clean and your utilization is managed.
- July: Pull your secondary bureau files (ChexSystems, LexisNexis, NCTUE). These should be clean if you completed Part Four work, but re-verify annually.
- October: Review all accounts for any late payments, incorrect balances, or status changes. Dispute anything that does not look right before it ages into your history.

Triggers for an Immediate Review

Pull your reports immediately any time:

- You receive an adverse action notice from any lender, insurer, landlord, or employer.
- You notice a hard inquiry on your report that you do not recognize.
- You receive a notice of a new collection account.
- You receive a data breach notification from any company that holds your financial information.
- Your credit score drops by 20 or more points unexpectedly.

Protection That Does Not Cost Money

Keep your credit frozen at all three major bureaus and all secondary bureaus at all times. Lift the freeze only when actively applying for credit, then refreeze within 24 hours of the application. This single practice eliminates the majority of identity theft risk without any ongoing cost.

Chapter 14

Business Credit: Building a Separate Financial Identity

Your personal credit is your personal credit. Your business credit is a separate credit profile for your business. Most small business owners do not know this distinction exists, and they end up using their personal credit to finance everything. That limits growth, exposes personal assets, and misses one of the best financial leverage tools available to entrepreneurs.

HOW BUSINESS CREDIT WORKS

Business credit is reported to business credit bureaus, primarily Dun and Bradstreet, Experian Business, and Equifax Business. These are separate from the consumer bureaus that track personal credit. A business can have excellent business credit even if the owner has damaged personal credit, and vice versa.

The primary business credit score is the Dun and Bradstreet PAYDEX score, which ranges from 0–100 and measures how promptly a business pays its bills relative to terms.

THE BUSINESS CREDIT BUILD SEQUENCE

1. Form a legal business entity. You need either an LLC or a corporation. A sole proprietorship tied to your personal SSN will not build true business credit.
2. Get an Employer Identification Number (EIN) from the IRS. Your EIN is the business equivalent of a SSN. Apply for an EIN free at www.irs.gov.

3. Open a business bank account. The account must be in the business name and EIN, not your personal name.
4. Register with Dun and Bradstreet. Get a Data Universal Numbering System (DUNS) number for free at www.dnb.com. This activates your business credit file.
5. Open vendor credit accounts. Net-30 vendors are companies that extend thirty-day credit terms to new businesses. Start with three to five vendors. Pay every invoice early or on time. These payments report to Dun and Bradstreet and build your PAYDEX score.
6. Move to store credit. Once you have a PAYDEX score, apply for business credit accounts at major retailers (Staples, Home Depot, Costco Business).
7. Move to revolving credit. With a solid PAYDEX and some history, apply for business credit cards that do not require a personal guarantee.

THE "HOW TO GET $5,000 IN CREDIT IN 90 DAYS" PLAN

This strategy works for people who need quick access to credit and are starting with a clean or rebuilding file.

1. Week 1–2: Open one secured credit card. Deposit $500 minimum. If your credit allows, open two cards at different banks. Total available credit: $500–$1,000.
2. Week 1–2: Apply for a credit union credit-builder loan. Most range from $500–$2,000. Total new credit: up to $2,000 available.
3. Week 2–4: Have a family member or trusted person with good credit add you as an authorized user on a card with a limit of at least $3,000. This card's limit now appears in your credit profile.
4. Day 60: With sixty days of perfect history and the authorized user boost, your utilization is low and you have three tradelines with positive history. Apply for one store credit

card (easier approvals than bank cards). Target $500–$1,000 limit.

5. Day 75–90: If approved for the store card, you may now be in position to apply for a small unsecured card from a bank. Target $500–$1,500.

Result at day 90: You can have $5,000–$7,000 in available credit across four to five accounts. Your payment history is perfect. Your utilization is low. Your score has improved materially.

Part Eight

Special Situations

Chapter 15

Identity Theft: What to Do When Your Credit is Hijacked

Identity theft is the fastest-growing financial crime in the United States. The 2017 Equifax breach alone exposed the personal data of nearly half the American population. If your identity has been stolen, credit damage is just one of several problems you are facing, but it is the one with the most systematic solution.

IMMEDIATE STEPS

1. Place a fraud alert with one of the Big Three. By law, they must alert the other two. A fraud alert requires lenders to verify your identity before opening new accounts.
2. Place a security freeze at all three major bureaus and all secondary bureaus. This stops new credit from being opened in your name immediately.
3. Pull all three credit reports. Look for accounts you did not open, hard inquiries you did not authorize, and changes to your personal information.
4. File an identity theft report at www.identitytheft.gov. This is the FTCs official identity theft portal. It generates an Identity Theft Report which is a powerful legal document. Bureaus must honor a dispute accompanied by an Identity Theft Report without requiring the standard thirty-day investigation.
5. File a police report with your local law enforcement. Some creditors require a police report number before they will remove fraudulent accounts.
6. Contact every creditor where fraudulent accounts were opened. Send a dispute accompanied by your FTC Identity

Theft Report and police report. Request immediate investigation and removal.

EXTENDED FRAUD ALERTS

A standard fraud alert lasts one year. If you are a confirmed identity theft victim, you can place an extended fraud alert that lasts seven years. To place an extended alert, you need to provide your FTC Identity Theft Report to the bureau.

THE FCRA BLOCK FOR IDENTITY THEFT

Under FCRA Section 605B, if you are a victim of identity theft, you can ask bureaus to block information that resulted from the theft, not just dispute it. A block is faster and more powerful than a standard dispute. The bureau must block the information within four business days of receiving your request accompanied by:

- A copy of your FTC Identity Theft Report
- Proof of your identity
- Identification of the fraudulent information

The FCRA block stops the information from appearing on your report. Furnishers are then notified that the information has been blocked due to identity theft and cannot continue reporting it.

SYNTHETIC IDENTITY FRAUD

Synthetic identity fraud is a growing problem where criminals create a new identity by combining real information (e.g., SSN) with fabricated information (fake name, fake date of birth, etc.). The resulting "synthetic identity" can be used to open credit accounts, and when it defaults, the damage can land in your legitimate credit file.

If you see accounts or inquiries in your file that appear to be for someone with a different name but your SSN, this may be synthetic identity fraud. Treat it as standard identity theft: FTC report, bureau disputes with FCRA block request, and police report.

Chapter 16

Credit and Housing, Employment, and Insurance

Credit reports and credit scores are used far beyond lending decisions. Understanding these non-lending uses helps you understand the full stakes of your credit health.

CREDIT AND HOUSING

Landlords routinely pull credit reports as part of the tenant screening process. Most residential landlords check at least one of the Big Three, and many also use specialty tenant screening services that pull CoreLogic or other specialty data.

What landlords look for:

- Rental history (specifically any prior evictions).
- Collection accounts (especially those from utilities or prior landlords).
- Overall credit score (most landlords want a minimum of 620–650).
- Public records.

If you have an eviction or rental-related collection in your history, you need to address it in the CoreLogic system, not just the Big Three. Many people clean up their Big Three reports and still get denied for apartments because the eviction is still sitting in CoreLogic.

Options if you have bad rental history:

- Offer to prepay several months of rent upfront to offset landlord risk.

- Provide additional references from previous landlords who can vouch for your reliability.
- Look for private landlords rather than property management companies with automated screening.
- Dispute any inaccurate eviction records in CoreLogic directly.

CREDIT AND EMPLOYMENT

Employers in most states can pull a modified version of your credit report (without your score) as part of a background check. They need your written permission before doing so. Federal law and many state laws require employers to give you a copy of the report before taking an adverse action based on it.

States that restrict employer use of credit reports include California, Colorado, Connecticut, Hawaii, Illinois, Maryland, Nevada, Oregon, Vermont, and Washington. If you live in one of these states, employers are significantly limited in how they can use your credit information.

If you are denied a job based on your credit report:

1. Request a copy of the report used.
2. Dispute any inaccuracies immediately.
3. Know your state's laws. In restricted states, you may have a legal claim.

CREDIT AND INSURANCE

Most auto and homeowners insurance companies use credit-based insurance scores to set premiums. These insurance scores are different from your lending credit scores, but they are derived from the same credit report data. Poor credit can mean paying significantly higher insurance premiums.

California, Hawaii, Massachusetts, Michigan, and Washington prohibit the use of credit in setting auto insurance rates. If you live in one of these states, your credit does not affect your auto insurance premium.

In states where credit-based insurance scoring is permitted, improving your credit can result in direct premium savings. Ask your insurer to re-run your insurance score after you have completed your credit repair work.

Chapter 17

Bankruptcy and Credit: The Truth

Bankruptcy has a reputation as a permanent financial death sentence. That reputation is wrong. Bankruptcy is a legal tool, and when it is the right tool for a situation, it can be the fastest path to financial recovery.

HOW BANKRUPTCY AFFECTS YOUR CREDIT

A Chapter 7 bankruptcy may remain on your credit report for up to ten years from the filing date under federal law. Chapter 13 may remain for up to seven years. The operative word is may. In practice, bankruptcies are frequently removed within two to three years through an active dispute process, particularly when the underlying accounts included in the bankruptcy cannot be independently verified by furnishers. Even when a bankruptcy record does remain, it generally does not prevent you from obtaining new credit within one to two years after discharge. Most lenders weigh your post-discharge credit behavior far more heavily than the bankruptcy itself.

However:

- After two years post-discharge, many lenders will consider you for credit with appropriate documentation.
- FHA mortgage loans are available two years after Chapter 7 discharge with rebuilt credit.
- VA loans are available two years after Chapter 7 discharge.
- Conventional loans through Fannie Mae or Freddie Mac require four years after Chapter 7 discharge.

Credit score recovery after bankruptcy is faster than most people expect. Within twelve to eighteen months of disciplined credit rebuilding, scores in the 650–680 range are achievable. Within thirty-six months, scores of 720 or higher are achievable for people who execute the rebuild strategy in Chapter 13 of this book.

DISPUTING ERRORS IN BANKRUPTCY REPORTING

Bankruptcy reporting generates its own set of common errors:

- Debts that were discharged in bankruptcy but continue to show as owed.
- Accounts included in bankruptcy not being marked as "included in bankruptcy" on all three bureaus.
- Incorrect discharge dates.
- Accounts associated with a spouse listed on a personal bankruptcy.

If your bankruptcy has been discharged and creditors are still reporting the debt as owed, that is a violation of the bankruptcy discharge injunction, which is enforced by the bankruptcy court. This is a serious legal matter beyond an FCRA dispute. Contact a bankruptcy attorney.

IS BANKRUPTCY RIGHT FOR YOU?

This book cannot answer that question for your specific situation. But here are the factors that typically make bankruptcy worth considering:

- Total unsecured debt exceeds your annual income and shows no realistic path to payoff.
- You are facing wage garnishment, bank levies, or judgment liens.
- You are behind on a mortgage and need the automatic stay to stop foreclosure.
- Medical debt has made your financial situation unmanageable.

Consult a licensed bankruptcy attorney before making this decision. Many offer free initial consultations. The means test calculation determines whether you qualify for Chapter 7 or must use Chapter 13.

Chapter 18

Debt Restructuring: The Alternative to Bankruptcy

Bankruptcy is a legal tool, and sometimes it is the right tool. But most people who consider bankruptcy have not fully explored debt restructuring first. Restructuring is the process of renegotiating the terms of your existing debt so that you can pay it back under conditions you can actually meet, without the ten-year credit stigma of a Chapter 7 filing.

This chapter gives you the full toolkit for debt restructuring so you can evaluate it as a real alternative before making an irreversible decision.

WHAT DEBT RESTRUCTURING ACTUALLY MEANS

Debt restructuring is not a single thing. It is a category of strategies. Depending on your debt type, your creditors, and your income situation, restructuring can mean:

- Negotiating a lower interest rate directly with a creditor.
- Extending the repayment term to lower monthly payments.
- Settling the debt for less than the full balance owed.
- Converting variable-rate debt to fixed-rate debt.
- Consolidating multiple high-interest debts into a single lower-interest obligation.
- Entering a formal Debt Management Plan through a nonprofit credit counselor.

None of these require a court filing. None of them produce a public record that follows you for a decade. And all of them leave you with more control than you have in a bankruptcy proceeding.

HARDSHIP PROGRAMS: THE FIRST CALL TO MAKE

Almost every major creditor has a hardship program that is never advertised. These programs exist because creditors would rather receive partial payment than no payment. When you call and explain that you are experiencing a financial hardship, a creditor can offer you:

- Temporary interest rate reduction, often to zero percent for six to twelve months.
- Waiver of late fees and over-limit fees.
- Reduced minimum payment requirements.
- Payment deferral for one to three months.

The key is to call before you stop paying, not after. Once you are sixty or ninety days behind, your account has typically been moved to collections, and the hardship options are more limited. If you see financial trouble coming, call the number on the back of your card the day you see it.

When you call, use these words: "I am experiencing financial hardship, and I want to discuss a hardship program before I miss any payments. Can you tell me what options are available?" That framing puts you in the cooperative borrower category and opens doors.

DEBT SETTLEMENT: THE NEGOTIATED PAYOFF

Debt settlement means paying a lump sum that is less than the full amount you owe, in exchange for the creditor considering the debt satisfied. Creditors will often accept 40–60 cents on the dollar for old or charged-off debt, especially when the alternative is no payment at all.

How it works in practice:

1. You stop paying the account (or it is already in default).

2. The account charges off and is either managed internally or sold to a collection agency.
3. You or a negotiator contacts the collector and makes a settlement offer.
4. If accepted, you pay the agreed amount in a lump sum or short installment arrangement.
5. The debt is reported as "settled" on your credit report.

Important realities about settlement:

- A settled account still damages your credit. "Settled for less than full amount" is a negative mark. However, it is less damaging than an open unpaid collection, and far less damaging than a bankruptcy.
- The amount forgiven may be taxable income. The IRS considers forgiven debt above $600 as income, and the creditor will issue a 1099-C form. Consult a tax professional before settling large amounts.
- Never settle verbally. Get every settlement agreement in writing and signed before sending any money.
- Once you pay a settlement, verify the update on your credit report within thirty days. Some collectors take the money and fail to update correctly.

DEBT CONSOLIDATION: ONE PAYMENT, LOWER RATE

Debt consolidation combines multiple debts into a single loan, ideally at a lower interest rate. The goal is to reduce the total monthly payment, reduce the interest burden, and simplify management into a single account.

Common consolidation vehicles:

- Personal consolidation loans from banks or credit unions. If your credit is good enough to qualify, this is the cleanest option.

- Balance transfer credit cards with a zero percent introductory rate. These can save significant interest if paid off within the promotional period, typically twelve to twenty-one months. Watch the transfer fee, usually 3–5 percent, and the rate that kicks in after the promo period.
- Home equity loans (HELOC) if you are a homeowner. These carry the lowest rates but put your home at risk. Use only as a last resort and only if you are confident in your ability to repay.

Consolidation does not reduce what you owe. It restructures how you owe it. If the underlying spending behavior that created the debt does not change, consolidation just delays the problem.

DEBT MANAGEMENT PLANS (DMP)

A DMP is a formal repayment program administered by a nonprofit credit counseling agency. The agency negotiates with your creditors on your behalf to reduce interest rates and waive certain fees. You make one monthly payment to the agency, which distributes it to your creditors.

Key facts about DMPs:

- They typically run three to five years.
- Your accounts are usually closed as part of the plan, which affects your utilization ratio and credit score in the short term.
- You cannot open new credit while on the plan with most programs.
- DMPs are reported to credit bureaus but are not as damaging as bankruptcy.
- Legitimate DMP providers are nonprofit and charge modest monthly fees, typically $25–$50. Avoid for-profit debt settlement companies masquerading as DMP providers.

The National Foundation for Credit Counseling (NFCC) maintains a directory of reputable nonprofit counseling agencies at nfcc.org. This is a legitimate resource.

RESTRUCTURING VERSUS BANKRUPTCY: THE DECISION FRAMEWORK

Use this framework to determine which path fits your situation:

1. If your debt is primarily student loans: Neither bankruptcy nor restructuring removes federal student loans easily. Income-driven repayment plans and Public Service Loan Forgiveness are your primary tools. Explore those first.
2. If your debt is primarily medical: Medical debt is being removed from credit reports under current bureau policies. Negotiate directly with the hospital for a zero-interest payment plan before considering any other option. Hospitals universally prefer payment plans to collection.
3. If your unsecured debt is manageable but rates are the problem: Consolidation or a DMP is the right tool.
4. If your debt is manageable but you are facing temporary hardship: Hardship programs from individual creditors are the right tool.
5. If your debt significantly exceeds your annual income with no realistic payoff path: Evaluate bankruptcy seriously. The credit damage is real but finite. The alternative is years of financial paralysis.
6. If you are facing foreclosure, wage garnishment, or bank levies: Bankruptcy's automatic stay provides immediate relief that restructuring cannot. Contact a bankruptcy attorney today.

Debt restructuring preserves your credit history, avoids a public court record, and keeps you in control. Explore every restructuring option before filing. But if the math does not work, bankruptcy is a legal tool, not a moral failure.

Chapter 19

Credit as a Launch Platform: Houses, Businesses, and Careers

Most people think about credit defensively: they want to avoid bad credit. That is the wrong frame entirely. The people who build real wealth in this country think about credit offensively. They use it as a launch platform.

I know this firsthand. By the time I was 21 years old, I had collected 1,000 credit cards and used them to buy and flip real estate. That is not a typo. One thousand credit cards. I understood something that almost nobody my age understood: credit is not debt. Credit is leverage. And leverage, properly used, builds wealth. Improperly used, it destroys it. The difference is knowledge and discipline.

This chapter gives you the framework I used and taught for forty years. Whether your goal is to buy your first house, launch a business, build a real estate portfolio, or establish career financing, the strategic use of credit is the accelerator.

THE 21-YEAR-OLD REAL ESTATE INVESTOR: WHAT I DID, AND WHY IT WORKED

In the late 1970s and early 1980s, the credit card market was less sophisticated than it is today. Issuers competed aggressively for card-holders, and approval standards varied widely. I studied the system. I understood that each card had its own credit limit, its own reporting cycle, and its own issuer relationship. I applied systematically. I built a portfolio of credit capacity the way a sophisticated investor builds a portfolio of assets.

When real estate opportunities appeared, I had liquidity. I could move fast. I could close deals that other buyers could not close because they were waiting on financing. Speed in real estate is worth money. The ability to act creates options.

The lessons from that experience are the foundation of this chapter.

PHASE ONE: GETTING YOUR CREDIT SCORE TO LAUNCH POSITION

You cannot launch from a damaged or thin file. Your first job is to get your score to a position where lenders will compete for your business, not question your credibility.

The minimum targets by use case:

- Credit cards for business use: 670 minimum, 700 preferred for premium cards with real limits.
- Business credit cards without personal guarantee: 700+ personal score plus established business credit history.
- SBA loan or business term loan: 680 minimum personal, with business financials to support.
- FHA mortgage: 580 minimum with 3.5 percent down, 500 minimum with 10 percent down.
- Conventional mortgage (best rates): 740 and above.
- Real estate investment property loan: 680–720 minimum, 25 percent down typically required.

If you are below these thresholds, Chapter 13 of this book (Building a Strong Credit Profile) and the dispute strategy in Part Six are your first priority. Get the foundation right. Everything else builds on top of it.

PHASE TWO: THE CREDIT CARD PORTFOLIO STRATEGY

A strategic credit card portfolio is not about getting cards to spend money. It is about building capacity, establishing history across multiple issuers, and creating financial optionality.

Here is how to build it:

1. Start with two cards at different issuers. Different issuers means different credit pulls and different relationship histories. Chase, American Express, Capital One, Citibank, and Discover each have their own approval criteria and their own internal credit systems.
2. Maximize limits over time. Every six months, call each issuer and request a credit limit increase. You are building total available credit, which is the raw material of low utilization ratios.
3. Maintain near-zero balances. High limits plus near-zero balances means ultra-low utilization, which is the engine of a high credit score.
4. Add business cards. Once your personal score is above 700, apply for business credit cards. Many business cards do not report to your personal credit file, meaning you can carry higher balances for business purposes without affecting your personal utilization ratio.
5. Use cards strategically for rewards. Travel points, cash back, and business expense rewards are real financial value when you are not paying interest. Pay every balance in full every month. Interest cancels every benefit.

PHASE THREE: BUYING REAL ESTATE

Real estate is the single most powerful wealth-building vehicle available to ordinary Americans. The combination of leverage (mortgage financing), tax advantages, appreciation, and rental income makes real estate unique.

How credit enables real estate:

The First Property

Your first home purchase is also your first real estate investment if you approach it correctly. FHA loans allow 3.5 percent down with a 580 credit score. Conventional loans allow 3–5 percent down with strong credit. That means for a $300,000 property, you need $9,000–$15,000 down, plus closing costs.

Where credit cards fit: Cash reserves for down payment and closing costs can be built over time using a disciplined savings strategy alongside your credit building. Some loan programs allow gift funds from families. Some allow down payment assistance programs at the state level. The mortgage itself is not where cards help. The preparation is.

The House Flip

Flipping properties requires capital that moves fast. Hard money lenders finance flips at high interest rates but quick closings. Your credit score matters to some hard money lenders and not at all to others, who focus on the deal itself.

Credit cards become a tool in flips for renovation costs. A $50,000 renovation budget funded partly through cards with zero-percent promotional periods can save substantial interest compared to financing everything through the hard money loan. The key is paying those balances off at sale, not carrying them forward.

The Rental Portfolio

Building a rental portfolio requires a credit score that makes conventional investment property loans accessible. Most investment property loans require 680–720 minimum and 20–25 percent down. Each additional property you buy improves your income picture for the next loan.

The portfolio strategy: Owner-occupied properties are the easiest entry point. Buy a duplex or triplex, live in one unit, rent the others. The Federal Housing Association (FHA) allows this structure with as little as 3.5 percent down. The rental income from the other units offsets your mortgage payment. After one year, you can move and convert the entire property to rental, then buy your next primary residence with another low-down-payment loan.

PHASE FOUR: STARTING AND FINANCING A BUSINESS

Starting a business without credit is possible. Starting a business with strong credit is faster, cheaper, and gives you more options at every stage.

Business Formation and Credit Setup

Do this in sequence:

1. Form your entity first. LLC or corporation. Not a sole proprietorship.
2. Get your EIN from the IRS (www.irs.gov, free and immediate).
3. Open a business bank account in the business name within the first week.
4. Get your DUNS number from Dun and Bradstreet (www.dnb.com, free).
5. Establish three to five vendor net-30 accounts in the first sixty days.
6. Pay every invoice early. Your PAYDEX score is built on payment timing.

Business Credit Cards as Operating Capital

Business credit cards are the most flexible, lowest-cost source of short-term operating capital available to small businesses. Used correctly, they provide:

- Float on expenses (thirty days interest-free between purchase and payment).
- Separation of business and personal finances, which is critical for taxes and liability.
- Rewards and cash back on business spending.
- A credit history for the business entity, separate from your personal file.

Target these business cards in sequence as your score and history allow: Starter business cards from your existing bank, then Capital One Spark, Chase Ink, American Express Business Gold or Platinum, and eventually cards with no preset spending limit for companies with established revenue.

Small Business Administration (SBA) Loans and Business Lines of Credit

Once your business has six to twelve months of operating history and your personal credit is above 680, you can access SBA loan programs:

- SBA 7(a) loans: Up to $5 million, used for working capital, equipment, real estate, and business acquisition. Rates are typically prime plus 2.75–4.75 percent. Personal guarantee required.
- SBA microloans: Up to $50,000 for small businesses and startups. Administered through nonprofit intermediaries. More accessible for newer businesses with limited history.
- Business lines of credit: Revolving credit facilities from banks. Drawn and repaid as needed. Usually require two years of business tax returns and 680+ personal credit.

PHASE FIVE: CAREER FINANCING

Career financing means using credit to fund the investments that increase your earning power: education, certifications, tools of your trade, or relocation to a higher-paying market.

Unlike consumer debt, career financing debt is an investment with a projected return. A $10,000 professional certification that increases your income by $20,000 annually is one of the best investments that exists. Evaluating the use of credit for career investment requires the same discipline as evaluating any business investment: what is the return, what is the timeline, what is the cost of capital?

Practical tools:

- Zero-percent promotional credit cards for education or certification costs paid off within the promo period.
- Credit union personal loans at below-market rates for career investments.
- Federal student loan programs with income-driven repayment for formal degree programs.
- HELOCs for homeowners making significant career or business pivots, using home equity at low rates.

THE 21-YEAR-OLD FRAMEWORK APPLIED TODAY

What I did at 21 was systematically study a system that most people ignored and exploit the opportunity it created. The credit system has changed since then, but the fundamental truth has not: most people use credit reactively. They borrow when they need something and pay as little as possible. The people who build wealth use credit proactively. They build credit capacity before they need it, deploy it strategically when opportunity appears, and manage it with discipline.

The person who reads this book and builds a 750+ credit score, a portfolio of low-interest credit relationships, and strong business credit before age 30 has access to a set of financial tools that most Americans never acquire in a lifetime. That is not an accident. It is a system. And now you have the system.

Credit is not debt. Credit is leverage. Build it before you need it. Deploy it when opportunity requires it. Manage it with discipline. That is the framework that built a real estate portfolio before I was old enough to rent a car.

Chapter 20

Getting Ready to Buy a House: The Complete Credit Preparation Plan

Buying a home is the single largest financial transaction most Americans will ever make. The difference between a 620 credit score and a 760 credit score on a 30-year $300,000 mortgage can be more than $100,000 in total interest paid over the life of the loan. Credit preparation for a home purchase is not a nice-to-have. It is one of the highest-return financial activities you can undertake.

This chapter gives you a specific, sequenced plan to get your credit in optimal position for a home purchase, whether you are twelve months out or thirty-six months out.

THE MORTGAGE CREDIT LANDSCAPE

Mortgage underwriting uses different scoring models and different standards than other credit products. Here is what matters specifically for home buying:

- Mortgage lenders pull all three bureaus and use the middle score of your three scores (or the lower middle score for co-borrowers).
- They use classic FICO versions: FICO 2 from Experian, FICO 4 from TransUnion, FICO 5 from Equifax. These are older models. Some behaviors that barely affect your FICO 8 score matter more in these versions.
- VantageScore 4.0 is being phased in under the Federal Housing Finance Agency (FHFA) mandate. As of 2026, some lenders are accepting it alongside classic FICO for conventional loans.
- Collections, judgments, and derogatory marks are scrutinized

heavily in mortgage underwriting even if they do not tank your score enough to disqualify you.

- Late payments within the last twelve months are a major red flag for most lenders, even a single one.

THE 36-MONTH PREPARATION PLAN

Months 36–24 Out: Foundation Work

At this stage, focus on:

1. Pull all reports from all bureaus and run the full dispute process from Part Six. Get every error removed now so the corrections have time to age and stabilize in your file.
2. Pay down credit card balances aggressively. Get total utilization below 10 percent and keep it there. This is the highest-leverage activity for score improvement at this stage.
3. Do not close any accounts. Length of history matters more in mortgage scoring models than in consumer scoring.
4. Do not apply for new credit unless necessary. Hard inquiries have more impact in the older mortgage FICO models.
5. If you have collections, begin the dispute and pay-for-delete process on any that are less than seven years old and more than $500.

Months 24–12 Out: Optimization

At this stage, focus on:

1. Check your scores quarterly. You are watching for the effects of your dispute work and your utilization management to show up in the classic FICO models.
2. Establish a savings history. Lenders verify not just your score but your down payment source. Most programs require that down payment funds be "seasoned" in your bank account for sixty to ninety days. Start accumulating and leave it sitting.

3. Clean up any remaining collection accounts. Medical debt under $500 should already be off all three major bureau files under current bureau policies. Focus on anything above $500.
4. Verify your income history. Mortgage underwriters need two years of W2 income or two years of self-employment tax returns. If you are self-employed, work with a tax professional now to ensure your returns reflect qualifying income.

Months 12–6 Out: Pre-Qualification Window

At this stage:

1. Get a mortgage credit consultation from a licensed mortgage loan officer or mortgage broker. This is not a full application. It is a credit review where they pull your file and tell you exactly where you stand and what needs to happen before you apply.
2. Correct any remaining issues the loan officer identifies. You now have a specific target list.
3. Freeze your secondary bureaus. By this point your Big Three disputes should be resolved. Freeze LexisNexis, CoreLogic, and other specialty bureaus.
4. Avoid any new credit. No new cards, no new loans, no financing anything.

Months 6–0 Out: Final Approach

In the final six months:

1. Stop all credit applications completely. Even a single new hard inquiry during this period can trigger underwriter questions.
2. Keep every existing account current with zero late payments. A single thirty-day late in the twelve months before application is a serious problem for most programs.
3. Do not close accounts or make any structural changes to your credit file.
4. Keep credit card balances as close to zero as possible, especially in the month before application. The balance that

appears on your credit report is the balance at statement close, not at payment due date.

5. Get pre-approved, not just pre-qualified. Pre-approval means the lender has pulled your credit, reviewed your income documents, and issued a conditional commitment. Pre-qualification is just an estimate based on self-reported information. Sellers take pre-approval seriously.

DOWN PAYMENT SOURCES THE RIGHT WAY

Your down payment must be documented and traceable. Lenders require sixty to ninety days of bank statements and will ask about any large deposits. Acceptable sources:

- Savings you have accumulated in a documented bank account.
- Gift funds from family with a signed gift letter and documentation of the transfer.
- Proceeds from the sale of an asset with documentation.
- Down payment assistance programs at the state and local level (search your state housing finance agency).
- Retirement account withdrawals or loans (with significant tax implications, consult a Certified Public Accountant, or CPA, first).

Credit card cash advances are not acceptable sources for down payments under most mortgage guidelines. This is a common misconception. The down payment must not come from borrowed funds.

WHAT TO EXPECT AT CLOSING

Even after loan approval, your credit will be pulled again shortly before closing, sometimes the day of closing, in what is called a "soft" or "hard" refresh. Lenders are checking that nothing has changed. Any new account opened, any large new balance, or any new derogatory mark between approval and closing can kill the loan.

Rules for the period between pre-approval and closing:

- Do not buy a car, furniture, appliances, or anything else on credit.
- Do not change jobs. Income stability is part of underwriting.
- Do not make large cash deposits without documentation.
- Do not co-sign any loans for anyone.
- Keep all existing accounts current and do not close anything.

The difference between a prepared buyer and an unprepared buyer is not luck. It is twelve to thirty-six months of deliberate credit management before you ever walk into an open house. Start that clock today.

Chapter 21

Negotiating with Creditors: Pennies on the Dollar and Full Deletion

The single most underused tool in consumer credit repair is direct negotiation. Most people assume that what a creditor says is what a creditor means. That assumption is wrong and expensive. Creditors, especially collection agencies, have enormous flexibility on both the amount they will accept and what they agree to report afterward. You just have to know how to ask.

This chapter gives you the full negotiation toolkit: the leverage you have, the tactics that work, the script to use on the phone, and the written agreement you must get before paying a single dollar.

THE DEBT MARKET REALITY: UNDERSTANDING YOUR LEVERAGE

Original creditors (banks, credit card companies, etc.) typically charge off a debt after 120–180 days of non-payment. At that point, one of two things happens: the creditor retains the account internally in a collections department, or they sell the debt to a third-party collection agency.

When debt is sold, the price is typically one to five cents on the dollar for older debt and five to fifteen cents for newer charged-off debt. A $10,000 credit card debt might sell for $150–$500. The collection agency that bought it for $300 is motivated to collect anything above that amount. An offer of $2,000 represents a $1,700 profit on a $300 investment. That is why collectors negotiate.

This is not a secret. Every debt collector knows it. You understanding it changes the conversation from a position of fear to a position of knowledge.

WHAT YOU CAN NEGOTIATE

You can negotiate two things simultaneously, and you should always negotiate both:

1. The amount. The settlement amount is typically negotiable to 20–50 cents on the dollar for most consumer debt. Older debt, debt with incomplete records, and time-barred debt negotiates lower.
2. The credit report outcome. This is the negotiation most people do not know to have. You are not just paying to make a debt go away. You are paying to make it disappear from your credit report entirely, to never be reported again. This is called a deletion agreement.

A "paid collection" still damages your score under most scoring models. A deleted account does not appear at all. The difference in credit score impact between paid and deleted can be 40–80 points. Always negotiate for deletion, not just settlement.

TACTIC ONE: THE SILENCE ANCHOR

The most powerful opening move in any negotiation is to say less than the other party. When a collector calls, do not volunteer information. Do not confirm the debt. Do not state what you can pay. Let silence create pressure. The collector will fill the silence with offers and concessions.

Opening script: "I am aware of this account. Before we discuss anything further, I need to know what your authority is to settle this account and whether deletion from all credit reporting agencies is available as part of any settlement." Then stop talking.

This single question does three things: it signals you know the system, it puts deletion on the table immediately, and it establishes that you will not be paying in full without getting something significant in return.

TACTIC TWO: THE LOWBALL ANCHOR

Whoever makes the first specific number in a negotiation establishes the anchor. Make that number yours, not theirs. Start with an offer of 10–15 cents on the dollar. It will likely be rejected, but it anchors the negotiation low.

Example: "I can offer you $400 as a full and final settlement on this account, provided you agree in writing to complete deletion from all three major credit reporting agencies and a commitment not to report this account to any bureau in the future. If those terms are acceptable, I can have a cashier's check or money order to you within ten days."

The lowball offer communicates: I have cash available, I am ready to close this now, and I know what I want. Collectors prefer quick closures over prolonged collections. The ten-day window creates urgency without pressure on you.

TACTIC THREE: THE WALK AWAY

The most underestimated power you have is the ability to end the conversation. Collectors know that a consumer who walks away may never come back. Walk away freely and repeatedly. "That does not work for me. I am going to move on. If your terms change, you can reach me in writing at this address."

Walking away signals that you are not desperate and not afraid of the debt. It almost always results in a better offer within days.

TACTIC FOUR: LUMP SUM VERSUS PAYMENT PLAN LEVERAGE

Lump sum payments are worth significantly more to a collector than payment plans. A collector who accepts a payment plan carries the account as an open liability with ongoing administrative cost and the risk you stop paying. A lump sum closes the file immediately.

Use this as leverage. A payment plan offer should always be for a higher total amount than your lump sum offer. If you offer $2,000 as a lump sum, a payment plan for the same debt should be $3,500 over twelve months. This incentivizes the collector to accept the lump sum, which is what you wanted.

TACTIC FIVE: TIME-BARRED DEBT LEVERAGE

If the debt is beyond the statute of limitations in your state, the collector cannot sue you to collect it. This dramatically reduces their leverage and dramatically increases yours.

For time-barred debt, your offer should be 5–15 cents on the dollar with a deletion agreement. If they refuse, point out that they cannot sue and that you will continue making no payments until they accept reasonable terms or the debt ages off your credit report entirely.

Critical warning: Do not make any payment on time-barred debt without first confirming your state laws. In some states, a partial payment restarts the statute of limitations. Consult an FCRA or FDCPA attorney if you are unsure.

THE PHONE CALL: WORD FOR WORD

When a collector calls, use this framework:

1. "I am aware of this account. I am prepared to discuss a resolution, but I want to be clear that any settlement must include complete deletion from all three major credit reporting agencies and a written agreement not to report this account in the future. Is that something you have authority to agree to?"
2. If yes: "Good. I can offer [lowball amount] as a lump sum final settlement. I will need the agreement in writing before any payment is made."
3. If they counter: "I understand. I need to think about that. Please send me something in writing outlining your offer and

the deletion agreement terms. I will review it and respond within five business days."

4. If they refuse deletion: "Then I am not interested in a settlement at this time. I will revisit when deletion is available." Then end the call.

Never pay while on the phone. Never provide a bank account or debit card number over the phone. Always require written confirmation before payment.

THE DELETION AGREEMENT: WHAT MUST BE INCLUDED

Before paying any settled amount, you must have a signed written agreement that contains all of the following:

- Your full legal name and account number.
- The original creditor name and the collection agency name
- The settlement amount (the exact dollar figure).
- A statement that the settlement is in full and final satisfaction of the debt.
- A specific commitment to "delete all references to this account from all three major credit reporting agencies within thirty days of receipt of payment."'
- A specific commitment that the account "will not be reported to any credit bureau or consumer reporting agency in the future."
- The name, title, and signature of the collector representative with authority to make this agreement.
- The date of the agreement.

Without every one of these elements, do not pay. A verbal agreement is unenforceable. An incomplete written agreement leaves you with no remedy if the collector takes your money and fails to delete.

AFTER PAYMENT: VERIFY THE DELETION

After your settlement check clears, pull your credit report from each of the three major bureaus within thirty days. Confirm that the account has been deleted, not just updated to "paid" or "settled." If the account still appears:

1. Contact the collection agency in writing and reference your deletion agreement.
2. Give them ten business days to complete the deletion.
3. If they fail to act, file a CFPB complaint attaching your deletion agreement and evidence of their non-compliance.
4. Consult an FCRA attorney. A collector who fails to honor a signed deletion agreement has potential liability.

The negotiation is not just about the money. It is about the paper trail. Get every agreement in writing. Verify every deletion. The signed deletion agreement is worth more than the settlement itself.

Chapter 22

Driving Records, Insurance Rates, and Your Right to Dispute

Most people do not realize that driving records and auto insurance reporting are governed by the same federal consumer protection framework that covers credit reports. The same rights that allow you to dispute a collection account allow you to dispute a driving record that costs you money on your insurance. This chapter covers both.

HOW DRIVING RECORDS AFFECT YOUR INSURANCE RATES

When you apply for auto insurance or renew a policy, the insurer typically pulls one or more specialty reports in addition to your credit file. These reports pull from multiple sources:

- Motor vehicle records (MVR) obtained directly from your state Department of Motor Vehicles, showing violations, suspensions, and license status.
- CLUE Auto (Comprehensive Loss Underwriting Exchange), operated by LexisNexis, which contains up to seven years of auto insurance claims you have filed or that were filed against you.
- Arity, operated by Allstate, which collects telematics data from mobile phone apps to score your actual driving behavior including speed, braking, and phone usage.
- Insurance Information Exchange (iiX), a Verisk company, which provides MVR data and employment screening for driving-intensive jobs.

A single at-fault accident or moving violation can increase your auto insurance premium by 20–40 percent for three to five years. Errors in any of these files can cost you hundreds or thousands of dollars per year in inflated premiums. You have the right to access and dispute all of them.

YOUR RIGHTS UNDER THE FCRA FOR DRIVING RECORDS

All specialty consumer reporting agencies, including insurance and driving record databases, are subject to the FCRA. This means:

- You are entitled to one free report per year from each agency. If an insurer takes adverse action against you (charges a higher rate, declines coverage) based on information from one of these reports, you are entitled to a free copy of that specific report within 60 days of the adverse action notice.
- You have the right to dispute any information you believe is inaccurate or unverifiable. The agency must investigate and correct or remove information that cannot be verified within 30 days.
- Information that cannot be verified must be removed, regardless of whether it is a credit account, a collection, or a driving violation in an insurance database.

HOW TO DISPUTE A DRIVING OR INSURANCE RECORD

The dispute process for specialty insurance and driving records follows the same core steps as a credit dispute. Contact each agency in writing, identify the specific item you are disputing, state why the information is inaccurate or unverifiable, and demand correction or removal. Keep copies of everything. Send certified mail, return receipt requested.

Equifax / LexisNexis CLUE Auto

Report request and dispute: www.risk.lexisnexis.com (click U.S. Consumer Reports) or call 1-866-897-8126. Mail: LexisNexis Risk Solutions Consumer Center, P.O. Box 105108, Atlanta, GA 30348-5108. Free annual report available. Security freeze available upon request.

Verisk A-PLUS Auto

Report request: www.verisk.com or 1-800-627-3487 (Option 2). Mail: Verisk Insurance Solutions, Consumer Inquiry Center, P.O. Box 5404, Mt. Laurel, NJ 08054. Free annual report available.

Arity (Allstate Telematics)

Report request: www.arity.com or 1-800-654-1412. Free annual report available if you have opted into any Arity data-sharing program through an insurance or app partner.

Insurance Information Exchange (iiX)

Report request: www.iix.com or 1-800-683-8553 (Option 6). Free report available upon adverse action notice.

THE TRAFFIC TICKET DEFERMENT STRATEGY

One of the most valuable and underused tools for protecting your driving record is the traffic ticket deferment program available in most states. Most people pay a ticket, accept the conviction, and do not realize that conviction will drive up their insurance rates for three to five years.

Here is how deferments work and why they matter:

What is a Deferment

A deferment, also called a deferred adjudication or a deferred prosecution, is an agreement between you and the court in which you pay a small administrative fee and agree to commit no additional violations for a defined period, typically 90–180 days. At the end of that period, if you have kept a clean record, the ticket is dismissed entirely. No conviction is entered. The violation does not appear on your driving record and does not appear on your MVR during the deferment period or after.

The financial impact of successfully completing a deferment is significant. A single speeding ticket conviction can increase your auto insurance premium by 20–40 percent. That increase typically lasts three to five years. On a $2,000 annual premium, that is $400–$800 per year, or up to $4,000 over five years. A deferment that costs $150 in court fees and an afternoon of your time can save thousands.

How to Request a Deferment

1. When you receive a traffic citation, do not simply pay it online. Paying a ticket is an admission of guilt that enters a conviction on your record.
2. Before the court date listed on your citation, contact the court clerk or appear at the listed hearing. In many jurisdictions you can also submit a written request for deferment.
3. Ask specifically: "I would like to request a deferred adjudication on this citation." In most states, first-time offenders are eligible for at least one deferment per period, often one every year or two.
4. The court will set a deferment fee, typically $100–$300, and a deferment period. Pay the fee and drive clean.
5. When the deferment period ends, contact the court to confirm the case is dismissed. Get a written confirmation. Keep it.

Deferments and Your Insurance Company

During the deferment period, there is no conviction on your record. An insurer pulling your MVR during that time will not see the violation. When the deferment is successfully completed, the case is dismissed and there is nothing to find.

If your insurance company asks about traffic violations, understand exactly what your policy requires you to disclose. A deferred ticket that results in a dismissal is generally not a conviction and does not require disclosure. If in doubt, consult a local traffic attorney who can advise you on the specific disclosure requirements in your state.

When Deferments are Not Available

Deferments are generally not available for serious violations including DUI or DWI, driving without a license, driving without insurance, reckless driving, and most commercial vehicle violations. They are primarily available for minor moving violations such as speeding, improper lane change, and similar citations.

AFTER A DENIAL: USING YOUR ADVERSE ACTION RIGHTS

If an insurer increases your premium or denies coverage based on information from a specialty report, the law requires them to give you an adverse action notice identifying the source. Use that notice immediately:

1. Request your free copy of the report from the specific agency cited within 60 days of the notice.
2. Review the report for errors, outdated information, or violations that were deferred or dismissed.
3. Dispute any inaccurate items in writing, certified mail.
4. If disputes result in corrections, request a re-rating from your insurer using the corrected report. Many insurers will adjust your premium retroactively.

The same rule applies to driving records as to credit: if it cannot be verified, it must be removed. Pull your CLUE report and your MVR annually. Errors in these files cost real money year after year.

Part Nine

The Future of Credit

Chapter 23

Where the Credit System is Headed

The credit reporting and scoring industry is undergoing the most significant transformation since its formation. Understanding where it is headed helps you make better decisions today.

OPEN BANKING AND CASH FLOW UNDERWRITING

Open banking refers to systems that allow consumers to authorize lenders to directly access their bank account data in real time with the consumer's permission. Rather than relying solely on credit report history, open banking-based underwriting looks at actual cash flows: income deposits, spending patterns, bill payment history, and account management behavior.

For credit repair purposes, open banking matters because:

- It creates an alternative path to credit approval for people with thin or damaged traditional credit profiles.
- Maintaining a well-managed bank account, with consistent deposits and no overdrafts, becomes a credit-building asset.
- Fintech lenders using cash flow data can approve borrowers that traditional credit models would decline.

ARTIFICIAL INTELLIGENCE (AI) AND MACHINE LEARNING (ML) IN CREDIT SCORING

AI/ML models can process far more data points than traditional statistical models. Some lenders are already using these models as supplemental or primary underwriting tools.

The credit bureau implications are significant: AI models can identify patterns in consumer behavior that traditional models miss. They can potentially score thin-file consumers who have been excluded from traditional credit markets. But they also introduce new risks of bias and opacity that regulators are beginning to examine.

DATA BROKER REGULATION

The CFPB proposed a rule in 2024 that would classify many data brokers as consumer reporting agencies under the FCRA. This would give consumers the right to access, dispute, and freeze data held by companies that currently operate entirely outside the FCRA framework.

As of this writing, this rule had not been finalized. The current regulatory environment has shifted toward less aggressive rulemaking. However, state laws, particularly California's CCPA and CPRA, are filling the gap. The long-term direction is toward greater consumer rights over data broker files, regardless of which federal administration is in power.

VANTAGESCORE IN MORTGAGE MARKETS

The FHFA's decision to allow VantageScore 4.0 in conventional mortgage underwriting alongside classic FICO is being phased in. This is a major shift with practical consumer implications:

- Consumers who score higher on VantageScore than FICO may find they qualify for mortgage financing they previously could not access.
- Consumers with non-traditional credit histories (thin files, recent immigrants, young buyers) may benefit from VantageScore's ability to score with less history.
- The competitive pressure between FICO and VantageScore may drive both companies to improve their models for consumer accuracy.

MEDICAL DEBT REMOVAL

The CFPB has been pushing to remove medical debt entirely from credit reports. The three major bureaus voluntarily removed paid medical collections and small medical collections in 2022 and 2023. A federal rule requiring removal of all medical debt from credit reports has been proposed. The future direction is clear even if the exact timing is uncertain: medical debt will play a decreasing role in credit scoring over the next several years.

TRIGGER LEAD RESTRICTIONS

When you apply for a mortgage, the bureaus sell that inquiry data to competing lenders immediately, who then bombard you with calls and offers. These are called trigger leads.

Legislation has been working through Congress to severely restrict or ban mortgage trigger leads. As of this writing, this legislation has strong bipartisan support. If passed, it will eliminate one of the most predatory uses of credit data that currently exists. Check for updates at your state's banking regulator website.

Chapter 24

Your Action Plan: The Complete Step-by-Step Timeline

This chapter gives you the complete execution roadmap. Follow it in order.

WEEK ONE

- Pull all three free credit reports from www.AnnualCreditReport.com.
- Pull your ChexSystems report.
- Pull your LexisNexis consumer disclosure report.
- Pull your Early Warning Services report.
- Pull your CoreLogic report if you plan to rent or have rental history.
- Pull your Innovis report.
- Create your master error log. List every negative item, which bureau it appears on, and the specific error.
- Place a security freeze at LexisNexis, ChexSystems, Early Warning, CoreLogic, Innovis, and NCTUE.

WEEK TWO

- Organize your evidence file. Gather ID, proof of address, payment records, and any relevant correspondence for the items you are disputing.
- Draft dispute letters for the highest-priority items at each of the Big Three. Limit to three to five items per bureau per letter.
- Send all dispute letters via certified mail with a return receipt.

- Log the date sent and the certified mail tracking number for each dispute.

DAY 30–40

- Review dispute results as they arrive from each bureau.
- Update your master error log with results.
- For deleted items, pull an updated report to confirm the deletion appears.
- For verified items you still believe are inaccurate, draft your escalation dispute directly to the furnisher.

DAY 40–60

- Send furnisher disputes for all items that survived the first round. Include your evidence.
- File CFPB complaints for any bureau that sent a verified result you believe was improper. Include copies of your dispute letters and the bureau response.
- Begin your credit building strategy in parallel. Open a secured credit card. Apply for a credit-builder loan at a credit union.

MONTH 3–6

- Review updated reports after furnisher dispute responses.
- If items still remain after the CFPB complaint route, consult an FCRA attorney.
- Continue your credit building: pay every bill on time, keep utilization low.
- Report rent payments if your landlord does not already report to bureaus.

MONTH 6–12

- Check your scores. You should see measurable improvement if negatives have been removed and positive history is being established.
- Once your score is above 650, consider applying for an unsecured credit card.
- Request a credit limit increase on your secured card if you have not converted to unsecured.
- Place security freezes at all three major bureaus now that your dispute process is complete.

MONTH 12 AND BEYOND

- Continue perfect payment history. One late payment undoes months of rebuilding.
- Maintain utilization below 10 percent.
- Do not close old accounts.
- Space new credit applications at least six months apart.
- Pull all reports annually to check for new errors or fraudulent activity.

Credit repair is a process, not an event. It requires consistency and discipline over time. But every person who executes this plan systematically ends up with a materially better financial life. That is the forty-year track record of this method.

Appendix A: Complete Agency Contact List

THE BIG THREE BUREAUS

Equifax

Consumer Reports: www.equifax.com or 1-800-685-1111
Dispute: P.O. Box 740256, Atlanta, GA 30374
Security Freeze: www.equifax.com/personal/credit-report-services

Experian

Consumer Reports: www.experian.com or 1-888-397-3742
Dispute: P.O. Box 4500, Allen, TX 75013
Security Freeze: www.experian.com/freeze/center.html

TransUnion

Consumer Reports: www.transunion.com or 1-800-916-8800
Dispute: P.O. Box 2000, Chester, PA 19016
Security Freeze: www.transunion.com/credit-freeze

SECONDARY AND SPECIALTY BUREAUS

Innovis

Consumer Reports: www.innovis.com or 1-800-540-2505
Security Freeze: www.innovis.com/personal/securityFreeze

LexisNexis Risk Solutions

Consumer Disclosure: www.risk.lexisnexis.com / consumerdisclosure
Opt-Out / Freeze: 1-888-497-0011

ChexSystems

Consumer Reports: www.chexsystems.com or 1-800-428-9623
Dispute: 7805 Hudson Road, Suite 100, Woodbury, MN 55125
Security Freeze: www.chexsystems.com / consumer-center

Early Warning Services

Consumer Reports: www.earlywarning.com or 1-800-745-1560
Security Freeze: www.earlywarning.com / consumer-information

CoreLogic

Consumer Reports: www.corelogic.com or 1-877-532-8778
Dispute: CoreLogic Credco, P.O. Box 509124, San Diego, CA 92150

NCTUE (National Consumer Telecom and Utilities Exchange)

Consumer Reports: www.equifax.com (managed by Equifax)
Reports available at 1-866-349-5185

MicroBilt/PRBC

Consumer Reports: www.microbilt.com or 1-877-243-5930

REGULATORY AGENCIES

Consumer Financial Protection Bureau (CFPB)

Complaints: www.consumerfinance.gov / complaint
Phone: 1-855-411-2372

Federal Trade Commission (FTC)

Complaints: www.ftc.gov/complaint
Identity Theft: www.identitytheft.gov

Annual Credit Report

www.AnnualCreditReport.com (free weekly reports available)

Appendix B: Sample Dispute Letter Template

[Your Full Legal Name]
[Current Address]
[City, State, ZIP]
[Date]
Dispute Department
[Bureau Name]
[Bureau Address]

Re: Formal Dispute of Inaccurate Credit Information

SSN Last Four: [XXXX]
Date of Birth: [MM/DD/YYYY]

To Whom it May Concern:

I am writing to dispute the following inaccurate information in my credit file. I request that you investigate this matter and correct or remove the inaccuracy in accordance with the Fair Credit Reporting Act, 15 U.S.C., Section 1681i.

Item Being Disputed:

Creditor/Collection Agency: [Name]

Account Number: [Last four digits if available]

Specific Inaccuracy: [Describe the error clearly and factually]

Requested Action: [Delete/Correct to reflect the following: describe correct information] I have enclosed documentation supporting my dispute including: [list documents enclosed].

Please investigate this matter and send me written notification of the results of your investigation within the timeframe required by law. If you cannot verify this information with the furnisher, please delete it from my credit file.

Sincerely,

[Signature]
[Printed Name]

Enclosures: [List documents]

Appendix C: Glossary of Key Terms

Adverse Action Notice

A notice required by law when a lender, employer, landlord, or insurer takes a negative action against you based on your credit report. It must state the reason and the bureau used.

Annual Percentage Rate (APR)

The yearly cost of borrowing money, expressed as a percentage. Includes interest and fees.

Charge-Off

When a creditor decides to write off a debt as a loss after you stop paying. Typically occurs after 120–180 days of non-payment. The debt still exists and can be collected or sold.

Credit Freeze/Security Freeze

A restriction placed on your credit file that prevents new creditors from accessing it. Free at all major bureaus.

Date of First Delinquency (DOFD)

The date when you first missed a payment on an account that eventually went negative. This date starts the seven-year clock for credit reporting.

Debt Validation

A debt collector's legal obligation to provide proof that a debt is valid and belongs to you when you request it in writing within thirty days of first contact.

e-OSCAR

The electronic system bureaus and furnishers use to exchange dispute data. Disputes sent to bureaus are transmitted to furnishers through e-OSCAR as automated dispute codes.

FCRA

Fair Credit Reporting Act. The federal law governing credit reporting, your rights, and the obligations of bureaus, furnishers, and users of your credit data.

FDCPA

Fair Debt Collection Practices Act. The federal law prohibiting abusive and deceptive practices by third-party debt collectors.

FICO Score

Credit scores created by Fair Isaac Corporation. Used in the majority of lending decisions in the United States. Multiple versions exist.

Furnisher

Any company that reports information about consumers to credit bureaus. Includes banks, credit card companies, auto lenders, student loan servicers, and collection agencies.

Hard Inquiry

A credit report accessed by a lender evaluating a credit application. Visible to other lenders, slightly lowers your score for up to twelve months.

Metro 2

The industry-standard data format furnishers use to report consumer account information to the bureaus.

Mixed File

A credit report that contains information belonging to a different consumer, usually because of similar names or SSN errors.

Re-Aging

The illegal practice of resetting the Date of First Delinquency on an old debt to make it appear newer and extend how long it can legally remain on your report.

Security Freeze

See Credit Freeze.

Soft Inquiry

A credit report access that does not affect your score. Includes your own inquiries, employer checks, and pre-approval screenings.

Statute of Limitations

The time period during which a creditor can sue you to collect a debt. Varies by state and debt type. After it expires, the debt is time-barred.

Tradeline

Any account that appears on your credit report.

VantageScore

A credit scoring model created by the three major bureaus as a competitor to FICO. VantageScore 4.0 is now accepted in conventional mortgage underwriting.

Appendix D: Complete Directory of Consumer Reporting Agencies

The following directory is sourced from the Consumer Financial Protection Bureau 2025 List of Consumer Reporting Companies. Under the Fair Credit Reporting Act, every agency listed here must provide you a free copy of your report if they have a file on you. You have the right to dispute inaccurate information and to place a security freeze at agencies that offer one.

This is not all-inclusive. The CFPB updates this list at www.consumerfinance.gov/consumer-tools/credit-reports-and-scores/consumer-reporting-companies/. You can submit suggested corrections or additions to CFPB_CCPD2@cfpb.gov.

NATIONWIDE CONSUMER REPORTING COMPANIES

These are the three primary nationwide credit bureaus used by the majority of lenders, landlords, employers, and creditors.

Equifax

Website: www.AnnualCreditReport.com | www.equifax.com
Phone: 1-888-378-4329 | In Spanish: Option 8
Freeze: 1-888-378-4329
Address: Central Source LLC, P.O. Box 105283, Atlanta, GA 30348-5283

Free weekly report available at www.AnnualCreditReport.com. Security freeze available at no charge.

Experian

Website: www.AnnualCreditReport.com | www.experian.com
Phone: 1-888-397-3742

Freeze: 1-888-397-3742
Address: Central Source LLC, P.O. Box 105283, Atlanta, GA 30348-5283

Free weekly report available. Security freeze available at no charge.

TransUnion

Website: www.AnnualCreditReport.com | www.transunion.com
Phone: 1-800-916-8800 | In Spanish: Option 2
Freeze: 1-800-916-8800
Address: Central Source LLC, P.O. Box 105283, Atlanta, GA 30348-5283

Free weekly report available. Security freeze available at no charge.

EMPLOYMENT SCREENING COMPANIES

Employment screening companies provide background check data to employers and volunteer organizations. Most will not have a file on you unless you have applied for a job and authorized a background check. Employment screening does not affect your credit score.

Accurate Background

Website: www.accurate.com | Phone: 800-784-3911
Address: 200 Spectrum Center Drive, Suite 100, Irvine, CA 92618

Free report available upon request if they have a file on you.

ADP Screening and Selection Services, Inc.

Website: www.adpselect.com (click Applicant Resources) | Phone: 888-606-7868 (Option 2)
Address: 2950 East Harmony Road, Suite 130, Fort Collins, CO 80528

Free report available for reports completed within the past two years. Older reports available by phone request.

Asurint

Website: www.asurint.com | Phone: 800-906-2034
Address: P.O. Box 14730, Cleveland, OH 44114

Free report available upon request.

backgroundchecks.com (a HireRight company)

Website: www.backgroundchecks.com | Phone: 866-265-6602
Address: P.O. Box 353, Chapin, SC 29036

Free report available upon request.

Blend Insights, Inc.

Website: www.blend.com | Phone: 855-520-1012
Address: 415 Kearney Street, San Francisco, CA 94108

Free report available if you recently applied for credit and your lender uses Blend. Security freeze available upon request.

CCC Verify (part of Experian)

Website: www.CCCVerify.com | Phone: 855-901-3099
Address: 50 Nashua Road, Londonderry, NH 03053

Free report available if your employer is a CCC Verify client.

Certiphi Screening

Website: www.certiphi.com | Phone: 800-260-1680
Address: Consumer Care Department, P.O. Box 541, Southampton, PA 18966

Free report available if they have previously run a background report on you.

Checkr, Inc.

Website: www.checkr.com | Phone: 844-824-3257
Address: One Montgomery Street, Suite 2400, San Francisco, CA 94104

Free report available if previously requested by one of their clients.

Cisive

Website: www.cisive.com | Phone: 855-881-0716
Address: 5000 Corporate Ct, Suite 203, Holtsville, NY 11742

Free report available upon request.

DISA Global Solutions, Inc.

Website: www.disa.com | Phone: 281-673-2400
Address: 10900 Corporate Centre Dr, Suite 250, Houston, TX 77041

Free report available upon request.

EmpInfo, Inc.

Website: www.empinfo.com | Phone: 800-274-9694
Address: 5900 Silver Creek Valley Road, San Jose, CA 95138

Free report available once every 12 months upon request.

Experian Verify

Website: www.experianverify.com | Phone: 866-312-8266
Address: P.O. Box 1971, Woodstock, GA 30188

Free report available if your employer is an Experian Verify client.

Fama Technologies

Website: www.fama.io | Phone: 888-748-3281
Address: 735 State Street, Suite 211, Santa Barbara, CA 93101

Provides social media screening. Free report available if they have a file on you.

Ferretly

Website: www.ferretly.com | Email: compliance@ferretly.com | Phone: 833-337-7385
Address: 16 N. Washington Street, Suite 102, Easton, MD 21601

Provides social media screening. Free report available by email if they have a file on you.

First Advantage Corporation

Website: www.fadv.com | Phone: 800-845-6004
Address: First Advantage Consumer Center, P.O. Box 105292, Atlanta, GA 30348-5292

Free report available once every 12 months. Security freeze available upon request.

HireRight

Website: www.hireright.com | Phone: 866-521-6995
Address: 14002 E. 21st Street, Suite 1200, Tulsa, OK 74134

Free report available upon request.

IntelliCorp Records, Inc. (subsidiary of Cisive)

Website: www.intellicorp.net | Phone: 888-946-8355 | Spanish: 866-202-1436
Address: 3000 Auburn Drive, Suite 410, Beachwood, OH 44122

Free report available once every 12 months upon request.

OPENonline (acquired by Universal Background Screening)

Website: www.openonline.com | Phone: 877-263-8033 (Option 1)

Address: 7127 South Riverside Pkwy, Tulsa, OK 74136

Free report available once every 12 months if previously requested by a client.

Pinwheel

Website: www.pinwheelapi.com | Email: fcra@getpinwheel.com
Address: 36 E 12th Street, Floor 2, New York, NY 10003

Free report available through Pinwheel portal if you have given your financial institution access.

Pre-employ.com, Inc.

Website: www.pre-employ.com | Phone: 855-940-3232 or 530-629-5296 (Option 3)
Address: P.O. Box 491570, Redding, CA 96049

Free report available if one has been prepared at the request of one of their clients.

Sterling (acquired by First Advantage)

Website: www.sterlingcheck.com | Phone: 888-889-5248
Address: 6150 Oak Tree Boulevard, Suite 490, Independence, OH 44131

Free report available once every 12 months upon request.

The Work Number (Equifax Workforce Solutions)

Website: www.theworknumber.com | Phone: 866-222-5880 or 866-604-6570
Address: Equifax Workforce Solutions, ATTN: EDR, 3470 Rider Trail South, Earth City, MO 63045

Free report available upon request. Security freeze available upon request.

Truework

Website: www.truework.com | Phone: 833-878-3967
Address: One Montgomery Street, Suite 2400, San Francisco, CA 94104

Free report available if your employer uses Truework.

Universal Background Screening

Website: www.universalbackground.com | Phone: 877-263-8033 (Option 1)
Address: P.O. Box 5920, Scottsdale, AZ 85261

Free report available once every 12 months upon request.

TENANT SCREENING COMPANIES

Tenant screening companies provide eviction history, rental payment data, and criminal background information to landlords and property managers. Most will not have a file on you unless you have applied for rental housing. A hard inquiry from a landlord can affect your credit score.

AmRent

Website: www.amrent.com | Phone: 888-898-6196
Address: AmRent Consumer Assistance, P.O. Box 530091, Atlanta, GA 30353

Free report available once every 12 months upon request.

AppFolio, Inc.

Website: www.appfolio.com | Phone: 866-359-3630
Address: 70 Castilian Drive, Goleta, CA 93117

Free report available upon request.

Contemporary Information Corp. (CIC)

Website: www.cicreports.com | Phone: 888-316-4242
Address: CIC Consumer Relations, 3700 Crestwood Pkwy
#300,
Duluth, GA 30096

Free report available after adverse action. Free eviction report available once every 12 months.

Experian RentBureau

Website: www.experian.com/rentbureau | Phone: 877-704-4519
Address: Experian RentBureau, P.O. Box 26, Allen, TX 75013

Collects rent payment history. Positive payments may appear on your Experian credit report. Free report once every 12 months.

First Advantage Resident Solutions

Website: www.fadv.com/resident-solutions | Phone: 800-845-6004
Address: First Advantage Consumer Center, P.O. Box 105292, Atlanta, GA 30348-5292

Free report once every 12 months. Security freeze available by request to consumer.documents@fadv.com.

Real Page, Inc./LeasingDesk (acquired by Thoma Bravo LP)

Website: www.realpage.com | Phone: 866-934-1124
Address: LeasingDesk Screening, 2201 Lakeside Blvd., Richardson, TX 75082

Free report available once every 12 months upon request.

RentGrow, Inc. (subsidiary of Yardi Systems)

Website: www.rentgrow.com | Phone: 800-898-1351

Address: RentGrow Consumer Relations, 68 Harrison Avenue, Suite 605, Boston, MA 02111

Free report available upon request.

SafeRent Solutions (acquired by Park Hill Holdings)

Website: www.saferentsolutions.com | Phone: 888-333-2413
Address: SafeRent Solutions Consumer Relations, P.O. Box 3890, Coppell, TX 75019

Free report once every 12 months. Security freeze available upon request.

Screening Reports, Inc. (division of BetterNOI)

Website: www.screeningreports.com | Phone: 954-526-6110
Address: 2900 Monarch Lakes Blvd., Suite 201, Miramar, FL 33027

Free report available if you submitted a rental application processed by them.

TransUnion Rental Screening Solutions/TransUnion SmartMove

Website: www.mysmartmove.com | Phone: 800-230-9376 (Option 4)
Address: TransUnion Rental Screening Solutions, P.O. Box 800, Woodlyn, PA 19094

Free report available upon request.

DEPOSIT ACCOUNT AND PAYMENTS SCREENING

Banks, credit unions, and merchants use these agencies to screen checking account applications and payment transactions. A negative record here can prevent you from opening a bank account. If denied an account, request a free copy of the report used.

Certegy Payment Solutions, LLC (owned by Variant Equity Advisors)

Website: www.askcertegy.com | Phone: 800-237-3826
Address: Certegy Payment Solutions, ATTN: CFDR Request, P.O. Box 908, Grand Junction, CO 81502

Free report available once every 12 months.

Chex Systems, Inc. (owned by eFunds/Fidelity National Information Services)

Website: www.chexsystems.com | Phone: 800-428-9623
Address: Chex Systems Inc., ATTN: Consumer Relations, P.O. Box 583399, Minneapolis, MN 55458

Free report and score available once every 12 months. Security freeze available upon request.

Priority: Freeze this first before the Big Three. A negative ChexSystems record can block you from opening any bank account for up to five years.

CrossCheck, Inc.

Website: www.cross-check.com | Phone: 800-843-0760
Address: CrossCheck Inc., ATTN: Consumer Inquiry Dept., P.O. Box 6008, Petaluma, CA 94955

Free report available once every 12 months.

Early Warning Services, LLC (co-owned by Bank of America, Capital One, Chase, PNC, Truist, US Bank, Wells Fargo)

Website: www.earlywarning.com | Phone: 800-745-1560
Address: Early Warning, ATTN: Consumer Services, 5801 N. Pima Rd, Scottsdale, AZ 85250

Operates the Zelle network. Also screens new banking applications at major banks. Free report once every 12 months.

Global Payments Check Services LLC

Website: www.globalpayments.com | Phone: 800-638-4600 (Ext. 410)
Address: Global Payments Check Services, ATTN: FACT ACT Support, P.O. Box 480357, Niles, IL 60714

Free report available once every 12 months.

TeleCheck Services, Inc. (subsidiary of Fiserv Inc.)

Website: www.firstdata.com/telecheck | Phone: 800-366-2425
Address: TeleCheck Services Inc., ATTN: Consumer Resolution Services, P.O. Box 6806, Hagerstown, MD 21741

Free report available once every 12 months.

PERSONAL PROPERTY INSURANCE REPORTING

Insurance companies buy specialty reports to set premiums and assess risk. Some collect telematics data directly from your phone or vehicle. If an insurer increases your rate or declines coverage, you are entitled to a free copy of the report used.

A-PLUS Property by Verisk (subsidiary of Verisk Analytics)

Website: www.verisk.com | Phone: 800-627-3487 (Option 2) or 800-709-8842
Address: Verisk Insurance Solutions, Consumer Inquiry Center, P.O. Box 5404, Mt. Laurel, NJ 08054

Collects home, auto, and property insurance claims history. Free report once every 12 months.

Arity (owned by Allstate Corporation)

Website: www.arity.com | Phone: 800-654-1412
Address: Arity, P.O. Box 227328, Dallas, TX 75222

Collects driving behavior data via mobile apps: speed, braking, phone use, mileage. Free annual report if they have a file on you. A file only exists if you opted into an Arity partner app.

Connected Analytic Services/CAS (affiliate of Toyota)

Website: www.connectedanalyticsservices.com
Email: fcranotice@connectedanalyticservices.com
Address: Connected Analytic Services, 7600 Windrose Avenue, Suite G-240, Plano, TX 75024

Collects driving data from Toyota vehicle telematics. Free annual report available upon ownership verification.

Drivers History (subsidiary of TransUnion)

Website: www.drivershistory.com | Phone: 855-694-1555
Address: Drivers History Consumer Relations, P.O. Box 600, Woodlyn, PA 19094

Provides driving violation records to insurance companies and employers. Free report after adverse action within 60 days of notice.

Insurance Information Exchange/iiX (subsidiary of Verisk Analytics)

Website: www.iix.com | Phone: 800-683-8553 (Option 6)
Address: Insurance Information Exchange, ATTN: Compliance Dept., 1574 Crescent Pointe Pkwy, College Station, TX 77845

Provides motor vehicle records and violation data to insurers and employers. Free report after adverse action.

LexisNexis C.L.U.E. and Telematics OnDemand

Website: www.risk.lexisnexis.com | Phone: 866-897-8126

Address: LexisNexis Risk Solutions Consumer Center, P.O. Box 105108, Atlanta, GA 30348-5108

CLUE maintains up to seven years of auto and property insurance claims. Free report once every 12 months. Security freeze available upon request.

MEDICAL REPORTING

These agencies report medical underwriting information to life, health, disability, and long-term care insurers. They generally will not have a file on you unless you have applied for individual (not group) life or health insurance.

MIB, Inc. (subsidiary of MIB Group, Inc.)

Website: www.mib.com | Phone: 866-692-6901
Address: MIB Inc., 50 Braintree Hill Park, Suite 400, Braintree, MA 02184

Collects medical condition and risk data for life, health, disability, and long-term care insurance underwriting. Free report once every 12 months.

Milliman IntelliScript (part of Milliman, Inc.)

Website: www.rxhistories.com | Phone: 877-211-4816
Address: Milliman IntelliScript, P.O. Box 2223, Brookfield, WI 53008

Collects prescription drug purchase history for life insurance risk scoring. Free report upon request.

LOW-INCOME AND SUBPRIME LENDING REPORTS

These agencies serve payday lenders, rent-to-own businesses, installment lenders, and other alternative credit providers. They are frequently missed by consumers during the dispute process and can cause denial of services even after the Big Three are clean.

Clarity Services, Inc. (owned by Experian)

Website: www.clarityservices.com | Phone: 866-390-3118 (Option 1: freeze; Option 4: report)
Address: Clarity Services Inc., Consumer Support Division, P.O. Box 16, Allen, TX 75013

Free report and score once every 12 months. Security freeze available upon request.

DataX, Ltd. (wholly owned by Equifax)

Website: www.datax.com | Phone: 800-295-4790
Address: DataX Ltd., P.O. Box 740125, Atlanta, GA 30374

Covers payday and installment loans, subprime credit cards. Free report once every 12 months. Security freeze available by mail.

FactorTrust, Inc. (owned by TransUnion)

Website: www.factortrust.com | Phone: 844-773-3321
Address: FactorTrust Inc., ATTN: Consumer Inquiries, P.O. Box 390, Woodlyn, PA 19094

Covers nonprime lending, short-term lenders, installment lenders. Free report once every 12 months. Security freeze available.

MicroBilt

Website: www.microbilt.com | Phone: 888-222-7621 or 800-884-4747 (Option 5)
Address: MicroBilt, ATTN: Consumer Affairs, P.O. Box 440693, Kennesaw, GA 30160

Collects rent, utility, phone, and streaming bill repayment data. Free report once every 12 months. Security freeze available.

Teletrack, LLC (owned by Equifax)

Website: www.consumers.teletrack.com | Phone: 877-309-5226
Address: Teletrack LLC, P.O. Box 740008, Atlanta, GA 30374

Serves payday lenders, rent-to-own, auto finance, cable/telecom companies. Free report once every 12 months. Security freeze available.

SUPPLEMENTARY CREDIT AND IDENTITY REPORTS

These agencies supplement traditional credit data with public records, property records, and identity verification data. They are used by financial institutions, insurers, healthcare providers, and government agencies.

Innovis (subsidiary of CBC Companies, Inc.)

Website: www.innovis.com | Phone: 800-540-2505 or 866-712-0021
Address: Innovis Consumer Assistance, P.O. Box 530088, Atlanta, GA 30353

The fourth major general credit bureau. Used for identity verification and fraud screening. Free report once every 12 months. Security freeze available.

LexisNexis Risk Solutions

Website: www.risk.lexisnexis.com | Phone: 866-897-8126
Address: LexisNexis Risk Solutions Consumer Center, P.O. Box 105108, Atlanta, GA 30348-5108

One of the most comprehensive files held on any consumer. Contains public records, property ownership, court records, professional licenses, bankruptcy and lien records, and historical addresses. Used by banks, insurers, employers, and government agencies. Free report once every 12 months. Security freeze available.

SageStream, LLC (owned by LexisNexis Risk Solutions)

Website: www.sagestreamllc.com | Phone: 866-897-8126
Address: SageStream LLC, LexisNexis Consumer Center, P.O. Box 105108, Atlanta, GA 30348-5108

Provides supplementary consumer reports to auto lenders, credit card issuers, retailers, utilities, and mobile phone providers. Free report once every 12 months. Security freeze available.

TELECOM AND UTILITIES REPORTING

National Consumer Telecom and Utilities Exchange (NCTUE) (managed by Equifax)

Website: www.nctue.com | Phone: 866-349-5185 | Dispute: 866-343-2821 | Freeze: 866-349-5355
Address: NCTUE Disclosure Report, Exchange Service Center, P.O. Box 105161, Atlanta, GA 30348
Freeze Mail: Exchange Service Center NCTUE, P.O. Box 105561, Atlanta, GA 30348

Collects and shares telecom and utility payment history including delinquencies and charge-offs for AT&T, T-Mobile, and other members. Free report once every 12 months. Security freeze available.

RETAIL RETURN FRAUD REPORTING

The Retail Equation (owned by Appriss, Inc.)

Website: www.theretailequation.com | Phone: 800-652-2331
Address: The Retail Equation, P.O. Box 51373, Irvine, CA 92619

Monitors and reports retail return and exchange fraud patterns to merchants. Free report available upon request.

GAMBLING AND SPORTS BETTING REPORTING

Central Credit, LLC (subsidiary of Everi Payments, Inc.)

Website: www.everi.com | Phone: 800-566-2087
Address: Everi Payments, 7250 S Tenaya Way, Suite 100, Las Vegas, NV 89113

Provides credit data to casino operators when extending lines of credit. Free report available upon adverse action.

NCC/National Cred-A-Chek, Inc. (owned by NRT Technology Corp.)

Website: nccreports.com | Phone: 800-421-2168
Address: National Cred-A-Chek, 3770 4th Ave, San Diego, CA 92103

Provides consumer data for gaming credit and fraud risk management. Free report once every 12 months.

VIP Preferred (a Pavilion Payments solution, owned by Parthenon Capital)

Website: www.vippreferred.com | Phone: 800-500-1973
Address: Pavilion Payments Gaming Services, Attn: FACT ACT Support, P.O. Box 480357, Niles, IL 60714

Serves casinos, sportsbooks, and racetracks for payment and cash advance risk assessment. Free report once every 12 months.

Source: Consumer Financial Protection Bureau, List of Consumer Reporting Companies, January 2025. The CFPB maintains the current version of this list at consumerfinance.gov. For complaints: 1-855-411-2372 or consumerfinance.gov/complaint.

Index

Page numbers are approximate and reflect the final typeset edition. All entries below reference the page on which primary discussion begins or resumes.

Note: Dan Kost, author—see also Author's Note (p. 4), About the Author (p. 369)

A

A-PLUS Property (Verisk insurance report) , 185, Appendix D

Adverse action notice, 73, 93, 185

AnnualCreditReport.com, 59, Appendix A

Arity (Allstate telematics), 259, Appendix D

Authorized user strategy, 151

Auto loans and credit mix, 25

B

Bankruptcy, Chapter 7, 195

Bankruptcy, Chapter 13, 195

Bankruptcy, removal before 10 years, 195

Big Three bureaus (Equifax, Experian, TransUnion), 35, 49

Business credit, 165

Business formation (LLC, EIN, DUNS), 165

C

California Credit Services Act of 1984, 4, 93

CFPB (Consumer Financial Protection Bureau), 85, Appendix D

CFPB complaint process, 85, 125

ChexSystems, 103, Appendix D

CLUE (insurance claims report), 185, 259, Appendix D

CoreLogic, 103, Appendix D

Credit bureaus, complete directory, Appendix D

Credit card portfolio strategy, 215

Credit freeze (security freeze), 15, 35, 59, 73, 103

Credit inquiries, hard, 25, 59

Credit inquiries, soft, 25, 59

Credit mix, 25, 151

Credit monitoring, free, 59

Credit repair, history of, 4

Credit Repair Organizations Act (CROA), 93

Credit score ranges, 25

Credit scores, types (FICO, VantageScore), 115

Credit Services Act of California 1984, 4, 93

Credit utilization, 25, 151

D

Dan Kost, 4, About the Author p. 369

Data brokers, 269

Date of First Delinquency (DOFD), 35, 49

Debt collectors, 139

Debt Management Plans (DMP), 203

Debt restructuring, 203

Debt settlement, 139, 203, 243

Debt validation, 139

Deletion agreement, 243

Deferments, traffic tickets, 259

Dispute letters, 125, Appendix B

Dispute process, step-by-step, 125

Driving records and insurance, 259

E

Early Warning Services (banking), 103, Appendix D

Equal Credit Opportunity Act (ECOA), 93

Equifax, 35, Appendix A, Appendix D

e-OSCAR dispute system, Appendix C

Experian, 35, Appendix A, Appendix D

F

FactorTrust, 103, Appendix D

Fair Credit Reporting Act (FCRA), 73

Fair Debt Collection Practices Act (FDCPA), 93, 139

FCRA Section 605 (seven-year rule), 49, 73

FCRA Section 605B (identity theft block), 175

FICO scores, all versions, 115

Free credit reports, rights, 59, Appendix A

Freeze, security, 15, 35, 59, 73, 103, Appendix D

Furnishers, 35, 73, 125

H

Hard inquiries, 25, 59

Hardship programs, 203

Home purchase preparation, 229

I

Identity theft, 175

Identity Theft Report (FTC), 175

Innovis, 103, Appendix D

Insurance and credit, 185, Appendix D

Insurance Information Exchange (iiX), 259, Appendix D

J

Judgments, civil (removed from Big Three 2017-2018), 49

K

Kost, Dan, 4, About the Author, 369

L

LexisNexis Risk Solutions, 103, 185, 259, Appendix D

Lump sum settlement, 243

M

Medical debt, 139

Metro 2 format, 35

MicroBilt/PRBC, 103, Appendix D

Mixed files, 35, 73

Money Smarts LLC, 4, About the Author p. 369

Mortgage preparation, 229

Motor vehicle records (MVR), 259

N

NCTUE (telecom and utilities exchange), 103, Appendix D

Negotiation tactics, creditor, 243

Negotiation script, word-for-word, 243

O

Open banking, 269

P

Pay for delete, 139, 243

Payment history (FICO weighting), 25

Pre-qualification (soft pull lenders), 59

Public records, 49

R

Re-aging of debt, 35, 49

Real estate investment and credit, 215

Rent reporting services, 115, 151, Appendix D

S

SageStream, 103, Appendix D

SBA loans, 165, 215

Score ranges, 25

Security freeze, See Credit freeze

Seven-year rule (FCRA Section 605), 49, 73

Soft inquiries, 25, 59

Statute of limitations, 139, 243

Subscription services, avoiding, 59

Synthetic identity fraud, 175

T

Tax liens (removed from Big Three 2018), 49

Teletrack, 103, Appendix D

Time-barred debt, 139, 243

Tradelines, 49

Traffic ticket deferments, 259

TransUnion, 35, Appendix A, Appendix D

Trigger leads, 269

U

Utilization rate, 25, 151

V

VantageScore, 115

Vendor net-30 accounts, 165, 215

W

Work Number, The (Equifax Workforce Solutions) , Appendix D

www.ingramcontent.com/pod-product-compliance
Lightning Source LLC
LaVergne TN
LVHW022023051126
851858LV00003B/28

* 9 7 8 0 9 1 6 5 3 9 3 8 2 *